CHOOSE GOOD FOOD
AND GOOD HEALTH

From Abalone to Zucchini, this authoritative book is your handy guide to the supermarket, restaurant, or kitchen—a one-volume course in nutrition that can save your arteries—and your life.

Studies have shown that a diet low in cholesterol and saturated fats can reduce the body's blood cholesterol and prevent heart disease.

Let these pages be your key to discovery: learn how different brands and methods of preparation affect the cholesterol content of food . . . plan balanced meals and menus that include your favorite foods. Give yourself and those you love the gift of vitality and good health.

THE
CHOLESTEROL
CONTENT
OF
FOOD

Corinne T. Netzer

A DELL BOOK

Published by
Dell Publishing
a division of
The Bantam Doubleday Dell Publishing Group, Inc.
666 Fifth Avenue
New York, New York 10103

For my friends at
The Pierre
C.N.

ISBN: 0-440-20176-4

Printed in the United States of America
Published simultaneously in Canada

August 1988

10 9 8 7 6 5 4 3 2 1

KRI

Introduction

WHAT IS CHOLESTEROL?

Cholesterol, an essential fatlike substance present in all animal life, is found among fats in the bloodstream. When cholesterol builds up in the lining of the blood vessels over a period of time, these blood vessels can narrow or close. If the arteries supplying blood to the heart, brain, or other crucial organs are blocked, the result can be heart attack, stroke, or failure of other vital organs.

The body gets cholesterol from two sources. Each day the liver manufactures about 1,000 milligrams of cholesterol, which is needed to produce certain hormones and to construct cells. The remaining cholesterol in the body comes from dietary sources. Because the body manufactures all it needs, it is the added dietary cholesterol which concerns us.

WHO SHOULD REDUCE CHOLESTEROL?

After an eighteen-month study, a federal health panel of twenty-two expert members concluded that large amounts of cholesterol can lead to heart disease, and that there should be an aggressive attack on high blood cholesterol to reduce the national risk. The panel warned that 40 million Americans have high cholesterol levels, placing them at high risk of heart disease.

The National Heart, Lung and Blood Institute report states that about 25 percent of Americans between the ages of twenty and seventy-four have high blood cholesterol and need treatment.

According to the National Institute of Health, approximately 1.5 million Americans suffer heart attacks each year, and 500,000 die.

GUIDELINES TO REDUCING CHOLESTEROL

The federal panel stated that the desirable blood cholesterol level is 200 milligrams per deciliter or less. The recommendation is that people with these readings have their cholesterol level rechecked every five years.

People with readings from 200 to 239 milligrams should be treated if they have other risk factors, the experts said. Other risk factors include being male, smoking, family history of heart disease, the presence of high blood pressure or diabetes, a history of stroke or blockage of blood vessels, and severe obesity.

Everyone with a reading of 240 milligrams or higher should be treated.

These recommendations were based on studies showing that every 1 percent reduction in blood cholesterol readings is accompanied by a 2 percent reduction in heart attack deaths.

THE RECOMMENDED DIET

The federal-recommended diet for reducing cholesterol starts with the *STEP 1 DIET,* which consists of reducing total fat in the diet to less than 30 percent of calorie intake, saturated fat to less than 10 percent of calories, and cholesterol to less than 300 milligrams per day. This diet is generally consistent with previous recommendations of the American Heart Association.

If the *STEP 1 DIET* fails to achieve the desired goals, the person is to be put on a *STEP 2 DIET* that reduces saturated fat to less than 7 percent of total calories and cholesterol intake to less than 200 milligrams per day.

If six months of dieting does not do the job, drugs are to be considered in addition to the diet. These drugs are unpleasant and may have severe side effects, so strict adherence to the diet is the best course in reducing cholesterol.

HOW THIS BOOK CAN HELP YOU LOWER CHOLESTEROL

The Cholesterol Content of Food is designed to take the guesswork out of cholesterol dieting.

Plan what you are going to have for the day, or even for the week. Then look up the cholesterol content—listings are arranged alphabetically for instant reference—and add up the figures. If you have chosen a 300-milligrams-of-cholesterol-per-day diet and you're over 300 milligrams, you will have to make an adjustment to decrease your cholesterol intake. If you have chosen the 200-milligrams-a-day diet and find you are over the alloted number of milligrams, you must make a similar adjustment. It's that simple. At first you may find it troublesome because many of the things we love most are high in cholesterol. But the benefits far outweigh the dietary inconvenience.

Lowering your cholesterol intake will lower your blood cholesterol count, but you should try to think of this as a new and better way of life, not just a stopgap temporary measure. I have, and I'm very proud of myself. You will be too.

CHOLESTEROL AND DIETARY FAT

Just because you look up a listing for a fat and it indicates that there is no cholesterol content does not mean that this is good for your diet. It is important for you to know that you should limit your intake of highly saturated fats because *they can raise your blood cholesterol level.*

Curtail your intake of coconut and palm oils, they are highly saturated. Also cut down on foods containing hydrogenated oils since hydrogenation makes fats more saturated.

You may see a product on your supermarket shelf that claims to be cholesterol-free because it uses only vegetable oil. Read labels. For instance, I'm sure you've read this listing on a box: "Contains one or more of the following: soybean, hydrogenated cottonseed and/or palm kernel oil." Listing all possible oils gives the manufacturer a choice when oil prices fluctuate. When presented with such a list, assume the worst, since saturated oils tend to be cheaper and have a longer shelf life.

THE DATA IN THIS BOOK

All information in this book is based on data supplied by the United States government or the individual producers and manufacturers.

As we go to press *The Cholesterol Content of Food* contains the most complete and up-to-date listings of cholesterol in food. In the future, as more information becomes available, I will be updating and revising this book.

Good luck and good dieting.

CORINNE T. NETZER

Abbreviations

diam. . . . . diameter
fl. . . . . fluid
lb. . . . . pound
mgs. . . . . milligrams
oz. . . . . ounce
pkg. . . . . package
tbsp. . . . . tablespoon
tsp. . . . . teaspoon
tr. . . . . trace
" . . . . inch
< . . . . less than

THE
CHOLESTEROL CONTENT
OF
FOOD

A

Food and Measure	Cholesterol (mgs.)

Abalone:
mixed species, fresh:
  raw, meat only, 4 oz. 96
  fried*, meat only, 4 oz. 107

Acapulco dip:
with American or Cheddar cheese *(Ortega)*,
  1 oz. 24
with Monterey Jack cheese *(Ortega)*, 1 oz. . . . 15
without cheese *(Ortega)*, 1 oz. 0

Acerola:
fresh 0

---
* *Flour-coated; fried in vegetable shortening*

Acerola juice:
  fresh.   0

Acorn:
  raw or dried   0

Acorn flour:
  full-fat   0

Ahi, see "Tuna, yellowfin"

Aku, see "Tuna, skipjack"

Albacore, see "Tuna, canned"

Alcoholic beverages, see specific listings

Ale, see "Beer, ale, and malt liquor"

Alfalfa seeds:
  dry or sprouted.   0

Allspice:
  ground   0

Almond:
  raw, dried, roasted, toasted, or smoked   0

Almond butter:
  plain, raw, or toasted.   0
  with honey and cinnamon   0

Almond meal:
  partially defatted.   0

Almond oil, see "Oil"

Almond paste:
  raw or toasted 0

Almond powder:
  full-fat or partially defatted 0

Amaranth:
  fresh 0

Anise seed:
  whole or ground 0

Apple:
  all varieties, fresh, canned, dehydrated, or
     dried 0

Apple butter:
  natural or cider 0

Apple cider:
  fresh, canned, or bottled 0

Apple danish:
  (Hostess), 1 piece 19

Apple juice or drink:
  fresh, canned, frozen, or mix 0

Apple rings:
  spiced, canned 0

Apple roll or bar:
 natural or sweetened 0

Apple sticks, fried:
 breaded, frozen *(Chill Ripe/Gold King* Fries),
  4 oz. 5

Apple-cranberry juice or drink:
 canned or bottled 0

Apple-grape juice:
 canned, bottled, or frozen 0

Apple-raspberry juice:
 canned or bottled 0

Applesauce:
 all varieties, fresh, canned, or in jars 0

Apricot:
 fresh, canned, dried, or frozen 0

Apricot kernel oil, see "Oil"

Apricot nectar:
 canned 0

Apricot roll or bar:
 natural or sweetened 0

Apricot-pineapple nectar:
 canned 0

Arby's:
sandwiches, 1 serving:

bac 'n Cheddar deluxe, 8 oz.	78
beef 'n Cheddar, 6.7 oz.	51
chicken breast, 7.4 oz.	57
hot ham 'n cheese, 5.7 oz.	50
roast beef, regular, 5.2 oz.	39
roast beef, junior, 3 oz.	20
roast beef, king, 6.7 oz.	49
roast beef, super, 8.3 oz.	40
turkey deluxe, 7 oz.	39
potato, baked, plain, 11-oz. serving	0
potato cakes, 3-oz. serving	13

potato, superstuffed, 1 serving:

broccoli and Cheddar, 12 oz.	24
deluxe, 11 oz.	72
mushroom and cheese, 10.5 oz.	21
taco, 15 oz.	45
French fries, 2.5-oz. serving	6

shakes, 1 serving:

chocolate, 10.6 oz.	32
jamocha, 10.8 oz.	31
vanilla, 8.8 oz.	30

Arrowhead:

fresh	0

Arthur Treacher's:

chicken, 2 pieces or 5.2 oz.	65
chicken sandwich, 5.5-oz. piece	32
fish, 2 pieces or 5.2 oz.	56
fish sandwich, 5.5-oz. piece	42
shrimp, 7 pieces or 4 oz.	93
chips, 4-oz. serving	1

Arthur Treacher's *(cont.)*
chowder, 6-oz. serving   9
cole slaw, 3-oz. serving   6
Krunch Pup, 2-oz. piece   25
Lemon Luv, 3-oz. piece   1

Artichoke:
globe or French, fresh   0

Artichoke, Jerusalem, see "Jerusalem artichoke"

Artichoke hearts:
fresh or marinated, canned, in jars or frozen . .   0

Asparagus:
fresh or canned   0
frozen, without sauce   0

Asparagus bean, see "Yardlong bean"

Au jus gravy:
canned, 10½-oz. can   1
dehydrated mix, .8-oz. packet   4
dehydrated mix, prepared with water, 1 cup . .   1

Avocado:
all varieties, fresh   0

Avocado dip, see "Guacamole dip"

B

Bacon, cooked:

4.5 oz. (yield from 1-lb. pkg. uncooked)	107
3 slices (20 per 1-lb. pkg.)	16
(Armour Star/Armour Low Salt), .3-oz. slice . .	6
(Armour Star/Armour Low Salt), .2-oz. slice . .	5
(Oscar Mayer), 1/5-oz. slice	5
(Oscar Mayer Center Cut),* 1/6-oz. slice	4
thick sliced *(Oscar Mayer),* 1/4 oz.	10

Bacon, Canadian, cooked:

4.9 oz. (yield from 6-oz. pkg. unheated)	80
2 slices (6 per 6-oz. pkg.)	27
(Armour 1877), 2 oz.	40
(Oscar Mayer), 1-oz. slice	12

Bacon, substitute, cooked:
  beef:
    6 oz. (yield from 12-oz. pkg. uncooked) 202
    3 slices (15 per 12-oz. pkg.) 40
    (Oscar Mayer Breakfast Strips), 2/5-oz. strip 13
    (Sizzlean/Firebrand), 2 strips 15
  pork:
    6 oz. (yield from 12-oz. pkg. uncooked) 179
    3 slices (15 per 12-oz. pkg.) 36
    (Oscar Mayer Breakfast Strips), 2/5-oz. strip 14
    (Sizzlean), 2 strips 20

Bacon bits:
  imitation 0
  real bacon *(Oscar Mayer),* 1/4 oz. 6

Bacon and horseradish dip:
  (Kraft) 0
  (Kraft Premium), 1 oz. 10

Bacon and onion dip:
  (Nalley's), 1 oz. 25

Bagel, frozen:
  plain or water 0
  all varieties, except egg *(Lender's)* 0
  egg, 1 bagel, 3½″ diam. 44
  egg *(Lender's),* 2-oz. piece 5

Baking powder:
  SAS, phosphate or tartrate 0

Balsam pear:
  leafy tips or pods, fresh 0

Bamboo shoots:
  fresh or canned 0

Banana:
  all varieties, fresh or dehydrated 0

Banana chips:
  dehydrated or freeze-dried 0

Barbados cherry, see "Acerola"

Barbecue dip:
  (Nalley's), 1 oz. 16

Barbecue loaf:
  1 oz. 11
  .8-oz. slice 9
  (Armour), 1 oz. 10
  (Oscar Mayer Bar-B-Q), 1-oz. slice 13

Barbecue sauce:
  meatless, in jars 0

Barley:
  pearled, light, pot, or Scotch 0

Basella, see "Vine spinach"

Basil leaves:
  fresh or dried 0

Bass:
  freshwater, raw:
    meat only, 4 oz. 77

Bass, freshwater, raw *(cont.)*
    1 fillet, 2.8 oz. (from 1-lb. whole fish)   54
   striped, raw:
     meat only, 4 oz.   91
     1 fillet, 5.6 oz. (from 2-lb. whole fish) 127

Bass, sea, see "Sea bass"

Bay leaves:
   fresh or dried   0

Bean curd, see "Soybean curd"

Bean dip:
   hot or onion *(Hain)*   0
   jalapeño bean, see "Jalapeño dip"

Bean flour:
   all varieties   0

Bean salad:
   all varieties, canned *(Joan of Arc)*   0
   marinated, canned *(S&W)*   0
   three-bean, canned *(Green Giant)*   0

Bean sprouts:
   all varieties, fresh or canned   0

Beans, baked, canned:
   with beef, 1 cup   59
   with franks, 1 cup   15
   with franks *(Nalley's)*, 3½ oz.   5
   maple sugar *(S&W)*   0
   meatless (vegetarian)   0

Beans, baked, canned *(cont.)*
with pork, 1 cup 17
with pork and tomato sauce, 1 cup 17
with pork and sweet sauce, 1 cup 17

Beans, barbecue:
and beef, canned *(Nalley's)*, 3¹/₂ oz. 5

Beans, black turtle:
dry or canned 0

Beans, blackeye, see "Blackeye peas"

Beans, broad, see "Broad beans"

Beans, butter, see "Butterbeans"

Beans, cannellini, see "Beans, kidney"

Beans, chili:
meatless, canned 0

Beans, fava:
dry or canned 0

Beans, great northern:
dry or canned 0

Beans, green:
fresh or canned 0
frozen, without sauce 0
dilled, canned *(S&W)* 0
seasoned, canned *(Del Monte)* 0

Beans, green, combinations, frozen:
and corn, carrots, and pearl onions *(Birds Eye)*   0
French, and cauliflower, and carrots *(Birds Eye)*   0
French, with toasted almonds *(Birds Eye)*   0

Beans, kidney:
red or white (cannellini), dry or canned.   0

Beans, lima:
raw or dry   0
canned or frozen, without sauce   0

Beans, mung:
dry   0

Beans, pea or navy:
dry or canned   0

Beans, pinto:
dry or canned   0

Beans, red:
dry or canned   0

Beans, Roman:
canned   0

Beans, shellie:
canned   0

Beans, yellow or wax:
fresh.   0
canned or frozen, without sauce   0

Beans, white:
dry or canned 0

Béarnaise sauce mix:
dehydrated, .9-oz. packet . . . . < 1
prepared with milk and butter, yield from .9-oz.
 packet 283
prepared with milk and butter, 1 cup 189

Beechnut:
raw or dried 0

Beef, retail cuts, edible portions:
brisket, whole, all grades:
    braised, lean with fat, 4 oz. 105
    braised, lean with fat, 11.4 oz.* 301
    braised, lean only (fat trimmed), 4 oz. 105
    braised, lean only (fat trimmed), 7.5 oz.* . . . 197
brisket, flat half, all grades:
    braised, lean with fat, 4 oz. 104
    braised, lean with fat, 11.3 oz.* 296
    braised, lean only (fat trimmed), 4 oz. 103
    braised, lean only (fat trimmed), 7.4 oz.* . . . 190
brisket, point half, all grades:
    braised, lean with fat, 4 oz. 108
    braised, lean with fat, 11.3 oz.* 304
    braised, lean only (fat trimmed), 4 oz. 108
    braised, lean only (fat trimmed), 7.7 oz.* . . . 206
chuck, arm pot roast, choice grade:
    braised, lean with fat, 4 oz. 112
    braised, lean with fat, 9.8 oz.* 274

* *Edible yield from 1 lb. raw as purchased (includes separable fat, connective tissue, and bone, if applicable).*

Beef, chuck, arm pot roast, choice grade *(cont.)*
    braised, lean only (fat trimmed), 4 oz. 114
    braised, lean only (fat trimmed), 7.1 oz.* . . . 203
  chuck, arm pot roast, select grade:
    braised, lean with fat, 4 oz. 112
    braised, lean with fat, 9.3 oz.* 263
    braised, lean only (fat trimmed), 4 oz. 114
    braised, lean only (fat trimmed), 7 oz.* 199
  chuck, blade roast, choice grade:
    braised, lean with fat, 4 oz. 117
    braised, lean with fat, 8.9 oz.* 260
    braised, lean only (fat trimmed), 4 oz. 120
    braised, lean only (fat trimmed), 6.5 oz.* . . . 193
  chuck, blade roast, select grade:
    braised, lean with fat, 4 oz. 117
    braised, lean with fat, 8.5 oz.* 248
    braised, lean only (fat trimmed), 4 oz. 120
    braised, lean only (fat trimmed), 6.3 oz.* . . . 188
  flank, choice grade:
    braised, lean with fat, 4 oz. 82
    braised, lean with fat, 9.5 oz.* 193
    braised, lean only (fat trimmed), 4 oz. 81
    braised, lean only (fat trimmed), 9.2 oz.* . . . 185
    broiled, lean with fat, 4 oz. 81
    broiled, lean with fat, 12 oz.* 241
    broiled, lean only (fat trimmed), 4 oz. 79
    broiled, lean only (fat trimmed), 11.7 oz.* . . 233
  ground, extra lean:
    raw, 4 oz. 78
    broiled, medium, 4 oz. 95
    broiled, medium, 11.9 oz.* 281

---

* Edible yield from 1 lb. raw as purchased (includes separable fat,
connective tissue, and bone, if applicable).

Beef, ground, extra lean *(cont.)*

broiled, well done, 4 oz.	112
broiled, well done, 9.9 oz.*	277
pan-fried, medium, 4 oz.	92
pan-fried, medium, 12 oz.*	274
pan-fried, well done, 4 oz.	105
pan-fried, well done, 10.4 oz.*	275

ground, lean:

raw, 4 oz.	85
broiled, medium, 4 oz.	99
broiled, medium, 11.4 oz.*	280
broiled, well done, 4 oz.	115
broiled, well done, 9.9 oz.*	283
pan-fried, medium, 4 oz.	95
pan-fried, medium, 11.5 oz.*	275
pan-fried, well done, 4 oz.	108
pan-fried, well done, 10.1 oz.*	273

ground, regular:

raw, 4 oz.	96
broiled, medium, 4 oz.	102
broiled, medium, 10.7 oz.*	273
broiled, well done, 4 oz.	115
broiled, well done, 9.6 oz.*	274
pan-fried, medium, 4 oz.	101
pan-fried, medium, 10.9 oz.*	273
pan-fried, well done, 4 oz.	111
pan-fried, well done, 9.8 oz.*	272

porterhouse steak, choice grade:

broiled, lean with fat, 4 oz.	94
broiled, lean with fat, 9.5 oz.*	222
broiled, lean only (fat trimmed), 4 oz.	91

---

* Edible yield from 1 lb. raw as purchased (includes separable fat, connective tissue, and bone, if applicable).

Beef, porterhouse steak, choice grade *(cont.)*

broiled, lean only (fat trimmed), 7.8 oz.* . . .	178
rib, whole (ribs 6–12), choice grade:	
broiled, lean with fat, 4 oz.	98
broiled, lean with fat, 10.2 oz.*	247
broiled, lean only (fat trimmed), 4 oz.	93
broiled, lean only (fat trimmed), 7.1 oz.* . . .	164
roasted, lean with fat, 4 oz.	96
roasted, lean with fat, 9.7 oz.*	234
roasted, lean only (fat trimmed), 4 oz.	92
roasted, lean only (fat trimmed), 6.6 oz.* . . .	149
rib, whole (ribs 6–12), select grade:	
broiled, lean with fat, 4 oz.	96
broiled, lean with fat, 10.1 oz.*	242
broiled, lean only (fat trimmed), 4 oz.	93
broiled, lean only (fat trimmed), 7.3 oz.* . . .	169
roasted, lean with fat, 4 oz.	96
roasted, lean with fat, 9.6 oz.*	230
roasted, lean only (fat trimmed), 4 oz.	92
roasted, lean only (fat trimmed), 6.7 oz.* . . .	153
rib, eye, small end (ribs 10–12), choice grade:	
broiled, lean with fat, 4 oz.	94
broiled, lean with fat, 11.6 oz.*	271
broiled, lean only (fat trimmed), 4 oz.	91
broiled, lean only (fat trimmed), 9.8 oz.* . . .	223
rib, large end (ribs 6–9), choice grade:	
broiled, lean with fat, 4 oz.	99
broiled, lean with fat, 10.2 oz.*	249
broiled, lean only (fat trimmed), 4 oz.	93
broiled, lean only (fat trimmed), 6.8 oz.* . . .	160
roasted, lean with fat, 4 oz.	96

---

* *Edible yield from 1 lb. raw as purchased (includes separable fat, connective tissue, and bone, if applicable).*

Beef, rib, large end (ribs 6–9), choice grade *(cont.)*

roasted, lean with fat, 9.9 oz.*	237
roasted, lean only (fat trimmed), 4 oz.	92
roasted, lean only (fat trimmed), 7.1 oz.*	161

  rib, large end (ribs 6–9), select grade:

broiled, lean with fat, 4 oz.	97
broiled, lean with fat, 10.1 oz.*	246
broiled, lean only (fat trimmed), 4 oz.	93
broiled, lean only (fat trimmed), 7 oz.*	164
roasted, lean with fat, 4 oz.	96
roasted, lean with fat, 9.9 oz.*	237
roasted, lean only (fat trimmed), 4 oz.	92
roasted, lean only (fat trimmed), 7.1 oz.*	163

  rib, short, see "short ribs," pages 31–32

  rib, small end (ribs 10–12), choice grade:

broiled, lean with fat, 4 oz.	95
broiled, lean with fat, 10.3 oz.*	244
broiled, lean only (fat trimmed), 4 oz.	91
broiled, lean only (fat trimmed), 7.8 oz.*	178
roasted, lean with fat, 4 oz.	96
roasted, lean with fat, 9.6 oz.*	231
roasted, lean only (fat trimmed), 4 oz.	91
roasted, lean only (fat trimmed), 6.9 oz.*	158

  rib, small end (ribs 10–12), select grade:

broiled, lean with fat, 4 oz.	95
broiled, lean with fat, 10.1 oz.*	240
broiled, lean only (fat trimmed), 4 oz.	91
broiled, lean only (fat trimmed), 8 oz.*	182
roasted, lean with fat, 4 oz.	95
roasted, lean with fat, 9.5 oz.*	227
roasted, lean only (fat trimmed), 4 oz.	91

---

* Edible yield from 1 lb. raw as purchased (includes separable fat, connective tissue, and bone, if applicable).

Beef, rib, small end (ribs 10–12), select grade *(cont.)*
    roasted, lean only (fat trimmed), 7.1 oz.* . . . 162
  round, full cut, choice grade:
    broiled, lean with fat, 4 oz. 95
    broiled, lean with fat, 10.7 oz.* 255
    broiled, lean only (fat trimmed), 4 oz. 93
    broiled, lean only (fat trimmed), 9 oz.* 208
  round, full cut, select grade:
    broiled, lean with fat, 4 oz. 95
    broiled, lean with fat, 10.7 oz.* 253
    broiled, lean only (fat trimmed), 4 oz. 93
    broiled, lean only (fat trimmed), 9 oz.* 209
  round, bottom (boneless), choice and select
    grade:
    braised, lean with fat, 4 oz. 109
    braised, lean with fat, 9.8 oz.* 266
    braised, lean only (fat trimmed), 4 oz. 109
    braised, lean only (fat trimmed), 9 oz.* 243
  round, eye of (boneless), choice grade:
    roasted, lean with fat, 4 oz. 83
    roasted, lean with fat, 12.6 oz.* 259
    roasted, lean only (fat trimmed), 4 oz. 78
    roasted, lean only (fat trimmed), 11.1 oz.* . . 218
  round, eye of (boneless), select grade:
    roasted, lean with fat, 4 oz. 82
    roasted, lean with fat, 12.7 oz.* 260
    roasted, lean only (fat trimmed), 4 oz. 78
    roasted, lean only (fat trimmed), 11.1 oz.* . . 219
  round, tip (boneless), choice grade:
    roasted, lean with fat, 4 oz. 94
    roasted, lean with fat, 11.6 oz.* 273

---

* Edible yield from 1 lb. raw as purchased (includes separable fat, connective tissue, and bone, if applicable).

Beef, round, tip (boneless), choice grade *(cont.)*
 roasted, lean only (fat trimmed), 4 oz. 92
 roasted, lean only (fat trimmed), 11.1 oz.* . . 233
 round, tip (boneless), select grade:
 roasted, lean with fat, 4 oz. 94
 roasted, lean with fat, 11.4 oz.* 268
 roasted, lean only (fat trimmed), 4 oz. 92
 roasted, lean only (fat trimmed), 10.1 oz.* . . 232
 round, top (boneless), choice grade:
 broiled, lean with fat, 4 oz. 96
 broiled, lean with fat, 11.7 oz.* 282
 broiled, lean only (fat trimmed), 4 oz. 95
 broiled, lean only (fat trimmed), 11.3 oz.* . . 269
 pan-fried, lean with fat, 4 oz. 110
 pan-fried, lean with fat, 10 oz.* 274
 pan-fried, lean only (fat trimmed), 4 oz. 110
 pan-fried, lean only (fat trimmed), 8.6 oz.* . . 238
 round, top (boneless), select grade:
 broiled, lean with fat, 4 oz. 96
 broiled, lean with fat, 11.7 oz.* 281
 broiled, lean only (fat trimmed), 4 oz. 95
 broiled, lean only (fat trimmed), 11.2 oz.* . . 267
 shank crosscuts, choice grade:
 simmered, lean with fat, 4 oz. 90
 simmered, lean with fat, 7.3 oz.* 165
 simmered, lean only (fat trimmed), 4 oz. . . . 88
 simmered, lean only (fat trimmed), 6.7 oz.* 147
 short loin, see "porterhouse steak" and
 "T-bone steak"
 short ribs, choice grade:
 braised, lean with fat, 4 oz. 107

Edible yield from 1 lb. raw as purchased (includes separable fat, connective tissue, and bone, if applicable).

Beef, short ribs, choice grade *(cont.)*

braised, lean with fat, 8 oz.*	212
braised, lean only (fat trimmed), 4 oz.	105
braised, lean only (fat trimmed), 4.3 oz.* . . .	114

sirloin, wedge-bone, choice and select grade:

broiled, lean with fat, 4 oz.	102
broiled, lean with fat, 10 oz.*	256
broiled, lean only (fat trimmed), 4 oz.	101
broiled, lean only (fat trimmed), 8.5 oz.* . . .	215

sirloin, wedge-bone, choice grade:

pan-fried, lean with fat, 4 oz.	111
pan-fried, lean with fat, 9.5 oz.*	265
pan-fried, lean only (fat trimmed), 4 oz.	112
pan-fried, lean only (fat trimmed), 7.3 oz.* . .	206

T-bone steak, choice grade:

broiled, lean with fat, 4 oz.	95
broiled, lean with fat, 10 oz.*	229
broiled, lean only (fat trimmed), 4 oz.	91
broiled, lean only (fat trimmed), 7.4 oz.* . . .	167

tenderloin (boneless), choice grade:

broiled, lean with fat, 4 oz.	98
broiled, lean with fat, 4.1 oz.**	100
broiled, lean only (fat trimmed), 4 oz.	95
broiled, lean only (fat trimmed), 3.6 oz.** . .	85
roasted, lean with fat, 4 oz.	99
roasted, lean with fat, 4.2 oz.**	105
roasted, lean only (fat trimmed), 4 oz.	97
roasted, lean only (fat trimmed), 3.4 oz.** . .	83

---

* Edible yield from 1 lb. raw as purchased (includes separable fat, connective tissue, and bone, if applicable).

** Edible yield from 5.7-oz. raw steak as purchased (includes separable fat, connective tissue, and bone, if applicable).

Beef *(cont.)*
  tenderloin (boneless), select grade:
    broiled, lean with fat, 4 oz.** 97
    broiled, lean only (fat trimmed), 4 oz. 94
    broiled, lean only (fat trimmed), 3.5 oz.** . . 84
    roasted, lean with fat, 4 oz. 99
    roasted, lean with fat, 4.2 oz.** 104
    roasted, lean only (fat trimmed), 4 oz. 97
    roasted, lean only (fat trimmed), 3.5 oz.** . . 85
  top loin (boneless), choice grade:
    broiled, lean with fat, 4 oz. 90
    broiled, lean with fat, 8.3 oz.*** 187
    broiled, lean only (fat trimmed), 4 oz. 86
    broiled, lean only (fat trimmed), 6.9 oz.*** . . 150
  top loin (boneless), select grade:
    broiled, lean with fat, 4 oz. 89
    broiled, lean with fat, 8.1 oz.*** 182
    broiled, lean only (fat trimmed), 4 oz. 86
    broiled, lean only (fat trimmed), 6.9 oz.*** . . 150

Beef, chipped, see "Beef, dried"

Beef, corned:
  (Carl Buddig), 1 oz. 16
  (Oscar Mayer), 3/4-oz. slice 8
  brisket, cooked, 4 oz. 111
  brisket, cooked, 11.3 oz. (yield from 1 lb. raw) 314
  canned, 1 oz. 24
  canned, 3/4-oz. slice 18
  jellied loaf, 2 slices or 2 oz. 24

** *Edible yield from 5.7-oz. raw steak as purchased (includes separable fat, connective tissue, and bone, if applicable).*
*** *Edible yield from 11.3-oz. raw steak as purchased (includes connective tissue and separable fat, if applicable).*

Beef, corned, hash:
  (Nalley's), 3¹/₂ oz.   35

Beef, cured, see specific listings

Beef, dried:
  2¹/₂-oz. jar   46
  1 oz.   18

Beef, ground:
  fresh, see "Beef"
  frozen patties:
    raw, 4 oz.   89
    broiled, medium, 4 oz.   107

Beef, roast, see "Beef"

Beef, smoked, see "Beef luncheon meat"

Beef brains, see "Brains"

Beef chow mein, see "Beef entrée, canned"

Beef dinner, frozen:
  Burgundy *(Dinner Classics)*, 10¹/₂ oz.   95
  Oriental *(Lean Cuisine)*, 8⁵/₈ oz.   35
  pepper steak *(Classic Lite)*, 10 oz.   60
  Salisbury steak, see "Salisbury steak dinner"
  short ribs, boneless *(Dinner Classics)*, 10¹/₂ oz.   95
  sirloin tips *(Dinner Classics)*, 11 oz.   100
  steak Diane mignonettes *(Classic Lite)*, 10 oz.   90
  steak teriyaki *(Dinner Classics)*, 10 oz.   95
  Stroganoff *(Dinner Classics)*, 11¹/₄ oz.   90
  Szechuan *(Classic Lite)*, 10 oz.   70

Beef entrée, canned:
chow mein:
  (Chun King Stir-Fry), 6 oz. with beef 52
  drained *(Chun King* Divider Pak/2 Servings),
    8.11 oz. 19
  drained *(Chun King* Divider Pak/4 Servings),
    7.14 oz. 17
  pepper Oriental, drained *(Chun King* Divider
    Pak), 7.05 oz. 15
pepper steak *(Chun King* Stir-Fry), 6 oz. with
  meat 51
stew *(Nalley's)*, 3½ oz. 20
stew, chunky *(Nalley Big Chunk)*, 3½ oz. 20

Beef entrée, frozen:
pepper Oriental *(Chun King* Boil-in-Bag), 10 oz. 23

Beef gravy:
canned, 1 cup 7

Beef kidney, see "Kidney"

Beef kidney fat, see "Suet"

Beef luncheon meat (see also specific listings):
Italian style *(Oscar Mayer)*, ¾-oz. slice 9
loaf, 1-oz. slice 18
smoked *(Carl Buddig)*, 1 oz. 16
smoked, chopped, 1-oz. slice 13
thin-sliced, 1 oz. 12
thin-sliced, 5 slices or ¾ oz. 9

Beef liver, see "Liver"

Beef spleen, see "Spleen"

Beef stew, see "Beef entrée, canned"

Beef tallow, see "Tallow"

Beef thymus:
  raw, 4 oz.   252
  braised, 4 oz.   333
  braised, 13.4 oz. (yield from 1 lb. raw) 1,119

Beef tongue, see "Tongue"

Beef tripe:
  raw, 4 oz.   107

Beer, ale, and malt liquor:
  all varieties, alcoholic and nonalcoholic   0

Beerwurst, see "Salami, beer"

Beet:
  fresh or canned   0
  frozen, without sauce   0
  Harvard or pickled, canned   0

Beet greens:
  fresh   0

Berliner:
  pork and beef, 1 oz.   13
  pork and beef, 1 slice, 2¹/₂″ diam. × ¹/₄″ . . .   11

Berries, see specific listings

Berry drink:
  canned or frozen   0

Biscuit:
  (Wonder), 1 piece   5

Bison, see "Buffalo"

Blackberries:
  fresh, canned, or frozen   0

Blackberry bar or roll:
  natural or sweetened   0

Blackeye peas:
  raw, dried, canned, or frozen   0

Blintzes, frozen:
  apple or apple-raisin *(Golden)*, 1 piece   28
  blueberry *(Golden)*, 1 piece   27
  cheese *(Golden)*, 1 piece   32
  cherry *(Golden)*, 1 piece   28
  potato *(Golden)*, 1 piece   19

Blood sausage:
  1 oz.   34
  1 slice, 5" × 45/8" × 1/16"   30

Bloody Mary cocktail:
  fluid or mix   0

Blue cheese dip:
  (Kraft Premium), 1 oz.   10
  (Nalley's), 1 oz.   13

Blueberries:
fresh, canned, or frozen   0

Blueberry syrup:
bottled   0

Bluefish:
raw, meat only, 4 oz.   67
raw, 1 fillet, 5.3 oz. (from 2-lb. whole fish)   88

Bologna:
(Armour), 1 oz.   15
(Oscar Mayer), 4/5-oz. slice   13
beef:
  1-oz. slice   16
  (Armour), 1 oz.   15
  (Oscar Mayer), 4/5-oz. slice   12
  Lebanon, 1-oz. slice   20
  Lebanon *(Oscar Mayer)*, 1.6 oz.   20
beef and pork, 1-oz. slice   16
cheese *(Oscar Mayer)*, 4/5-oz. slice   14
garlic *(Oscar Mayer)*, 4/5-oz. slice   13
meat *(Armour)*, 1 oz.   15
pork, 1 oz.   17
pork, .8-oz. slice   14
turkey, see "Turkey bologna"

Borage:
fresh   0

Bouillon:
beef or chicken, see "Soup"
onion or vegetable, cubes or powder   0

Bourbon, see "Liquor"

Boysenberries:
fresh, canned, or frozen 0

Boysenberry juice:
bottled 0

Brains:
beef, braised, 4 oz. 2,329
beef, pan-fried, 4 oz. 2,262
pork, braised, 4 oz. 2,894

Bran, see specific listings and "Cereal, ready-to-eat"

Brandy, see "Liquor"

Bratwurst:
cooked *(Hillshire Farm),* 1 oz. 8
pork, cooked, 1 oz. 17
pork, cooked, 1 link (4 per 12-oz. pkg.) 51
pork and beef, 1 oz. 18
pork and beef, 1 link (7 per lb.) 44

Braunschweiger:
(Oscar Mayer), 1-oz. slice 50
(Oscar Mayer Chub), 1 oz. 46
(Oscar Mayer Tube), 1 oz. 41
pork, 1 oz. 44
pork, 1 slice, 2½" diam. × ¼" 28

Brazil nuts:
raw or dried 0

Bread:

(Arnold Bran'nola)	0
bran, honey *(Freihofer's)*, 2 slices	< 5
bran, honey *(Roman Meal)*	0
(Freihofer's/Freihofer's Old Fashion)	0
(Freihofer's Low Sodium), 2 slices	< 5
French:	
(DiCarlo Parisian), 1 slice	< 5
(Gonnella)	0
(Wonder)	0
(Hillbilly), 1 slice	< 5
(Hollywood Dark or Light), 1 slice	< 5
Italian *(Freihofer's/Freihofer's Pane Italian)*,	
2 slices	< 5
Italian *(Wonder Family)*, 1 slice	< 5
(Monk's Hi-Fibre)	0
multi-grain *(Home Pride 7 Grain)*, 1 slice	< 5
multi-grain *(Roman Seven Grain)*	0
oat *(Arnold Bran'nola Country)*, 2 slices	< 5
oat *(Freihofer's Canadian Oat)*, 2 slices	< 5
pita *(Sahara Regular or Whole Wheat)*	0
protein *(Thomas' Fresh or Frozen)*	0
pumpernickel:	
(Arnold)	0
(Freihofer's Bavarian), 2 slices	< 5
(Levy's)	0
raisin *(Arnold Tea)*, 2 slices	< 5
raisin *(Monk's)*	0
(Roman Meal), 1 slice	< 5
rye:	
(Arnold Melba Thin)	0
dill *(Arnold)*	0
Jewish, seeded *(Arnold)*, 2 slices	< 5
Jewish, seeded *(Levy's)*	0

Bread, rye *(cont.)*

soft *(Freihofer's)*, 2 slices . . . .   < 5

sourdough, French:

  (Boudin), 2 slices or 1¾ oz. . . . .   tr.

  (DiCarlo)   0

  (Parisian), 1.8 oz. . . . .   tr.

wheat:

  (Arnold Bran'nola Hearty), 2 slices . . . . . .   < 5

  (Freihofer's Buttercrust/Split Top), 2 slices   < 5

  (Fresh Horizons)   0

  (Fresh & Natural)   0

  (Home Pride Butter Top/Wheatberry), 1 slice   < 5

  (Monk's)   0

  (Roman Meal Light), 1 slice . . . .   < 5

  (Roman Wheatberry)   0

  (Wonder Family), 1 slice . . . .   < 5

  cracked *(Freihofer's)*, 2 slices . . . .   < 5

  cracked *(Roman Meal)*   0

  cracked *(Wonder)*, 1 slice . . . .   < 5

  honey *(Arnold* Wheatberry), 2 slices . . . . . .   < 5

  sprouted *(Arnold)*, 2 slices . . . .   < 5

  whole *(Arnold* Brick Oven), 2 slices . . . . . .   < 5

  whole *(Arnold* Measure Up), 2 slices . . . . . .   < 5

  whole *(Roman Meal* 100% Whole Grain) . . .   0

  whole *(Wonder* 100%), 1 slice . . . .   < 5

  whole, soft *(Wonder* 100%)   0

white:

  (Arnold Bran'nola Old Style)   0

  (Arnold Brick Oven), 2 slices . . . .   < 5

  (Arnold Country), 2 slices . . . .   < 5

  (Arnold Hearthstone)   0

  (Arnold Measure Up), 2 slices . . . .   < 5

  (Freihofer's/Freihofer's Buttercrust), 2 slices   < 5

  (Freihofer's Split Top)   0

Bread, white *(cont.)*
   (Fresh Horizons) 0
   (Home Pride Butter Top), 1 slice . . . . < 5
   (Monk's) 0
   (Roman Meal Light), 1 slice . . . . < 5
   (Wonder), 1 slice . . . . < 5
   with buttermilk *(Wonder)*, 1 slice . . . . < 5
  Vienna *(Gonnella)* 0

Bread crumbs:
  dry, grated, 1 cup 5
  soft, white bread 0
  seasoned *(Contadina)* 0
  toasted *(Old London)* 0

Bread dough:
  white bread, frozen *(Rich's)* 0

Bread stuffing, see "Stuffing mix"

Breadfruit:
  fresh 0

Breadfruit seeds:
  raw or toasted 0

Breadnut tree seeds:
  raw or dried 0

Breakfast strips, see "Bacon, substitute"

Broad beans:
  raw or dried 0

Broccoli:
fresh. 0
frozen, without sauce 0

Broccoli combinations, frozen:
and baby carrots and water chestnuts *(Birds Eye)* 0
and carrot fanfare *(Green Giant Valley Combination)* 0
and cauliflower *(Kohl's)* 0
and cauliflower supreme *(Green Giant Valley Combination)* 0
and cauliflower and carrots *(Birds Eye)* 0
and corn and red peppers *(Birds Eye)* 0
and green beans, pearl onions, and red peppers *(Birds Eye)* 0
and water chestnuts *(Birds Eye)* 0

Brown gravy mix:
dehydrated, .9-oz. packet. 2
dehydrated, prepared with water, 1 cup . . . . . tr.
(Spatini Family Style) 0

Brownie, see "Cookies"

Browning sauce:
(Gravy Master) 0

Brussels sprouts:
fresh. 0
frozen, without sauce 0
with cauliflower and carrots, frozen *(Birds Eye)* 0

Buckwheat flour, see "Flour"

Buffalo:
raw, lean meat only, 4 oz. 70

Bulgur:
all wheat varieties 0
canned, seasoned or unseasoned 0

Bun, honey:
glazed *(Hostess)*, 1 piece 24

Burbot:
fresh, raw, meat only, 4 oz. 68
fresh, raw, 4.1-oz. fillet (from 1½-lb. whole
   fish) 69

Burdock root:
fresh 0

Burrito sauce:
canned *(Del Monte* Salsa) 0

Butter:
regular:
   4 oz., 1 stick or ½ cup 248
   1 tbsp. 31
   1 tsp. 10
   1 pat, 1″ × ⅓″ 11
whipped:
   ½ cup or 1 stick 165
   1 tbsp. 20
   1 tsp. 7
   1 pat, 1¼″ × ⅓″ 8

Butter oil:
  1 tbsp.   33

Butterbeans:
  canned or frozen   0

Butterbur:
  fresh   0

Butterfish:
  raw, meat only, 4 oz.   74
  raw, 1 fillet, 1.1 oz. (from 1/2-lb. whole fish) . . .   21

Butterhorn danish:
  (Hostess), 1 piece   8

Buttermilk, see "Milk"

Buttermilk dip:
  (Kraft)   0

Butternuts:
  raw or dried   0

C

Food and Measure	Cholesterol (mgs.)
Cabbage:	
white or red, fresh or canned	0
Cabbage, Chinese:	
fresh	0
Cabbage, savoy:	
fresh	0
Cabbage, stuffed, dinner, frozen:	
(Classic Lite), 12 oz.	40
(Lean Cuisine), 10¾ oz.	40
Cake, commercial:	
cheese cake, 9″-diam. cake	2053
cheese cake, 1/12 of 9″-diam. cake	170

Cake, commercial *(cont.)*
pound cake, 1 loaf, 8½" × 3½" × 3" 1100
pound cake, 1/17 of 8½" loaf 64
white, with white frosting:
2-layer, 8"–9"-diam. cake 46
2-layer, 1/16 of 8"–9"-diam. cake 3
yellow, with chocolate frosting:
2-layer, 8"–9"-diam. cake 609
2-layer, 1/16 of 8"–9"-diam. cake 38

Cake, mix* :
angel food 0
coffee cake, crumb, 1 cake, 7¾" × 5⅝"
×1¼" 279
coffee cake, crumb, 1/6 of 7¾" cake 47
devil's food, with chocolate frosting:
2-layer, 8"–9"-diam. cake 598
2-layer, 1/16 of 8"–9"-diam. cake 37
cupcake, 2½" diam. 19
gingerbread, 8"-square cake 6
gingerbread, 1/9 of 8"-square cake 1
yellow, with chocolate frosting:
2-layer, 8"–9"-diam. cake 576
2-layer, 1/16 of 8"–9"-diam. cake 36

Cake, snack:
banana *(Hostess Suzy Q's)*, 1 piece 21
chocolate or devil's food:
creme filled, 1 small piece (2 per pkg.) 15
(Hostess Big Wheels), 1 piece 6
(Hostess Chip Flips), 1 piece 25
(Hostess Choco-Diles), 1 piece 22

_____
* *Prepared according to package directions*

Cake, snack, chocolate or devil's food *(cont.)*
   (Hostess Ding Dongs), 1 piece   6
   (Hostess Ho Hos), 1 piece   13
   (Hostess Suzy Q's), 1 piece   16
   coconut covered *(Hostess Sno Balls)*,
     1 piece   2
   cupcake:
     chocolate *(Hostess)*, 1 piece   3
     (Hostess Dessert Cups), 1 piece   9
     orange *(Hostess)*, 1 piece   13
   (Hostess L'il Angels), 1 piece   2
   (Hostess O's), 1 piece   14
   (Hostess Tiger Tails), 1 piece   25
   (Hostess Twinkies), 1 piece   20
   peanut, plain or filled *(Hostess Peanut Putters)*,
     1 piece   4
   sponge cake, creme filled, 1 small piece (2 per
     pkg.)   7

Candy:
   butterscotch chips *(Nestlé* Morsels)   0
   candy corn, see "fondant," below
   caramel, plain or chocolate, 1 oz.   1
   caramel *(Kraft)*   0
   chocolate:
     (Estee Bar), 2 squares   2
     with crisps *(Estee)*, 2 squares   2
     dark or sweet   0
     fudgie *(Kraft)*   0
     milk, 1 oz.   6
     milk *(Andes* Petite), 1 oz. . . . .   < 4
     milk, with almonds, 1 oz.   5
     milk, with crisps (rice cereal), 1 oz.   6
     milk, with crisps *(Nestlé* Crunch) 1 1/16-oz. bar   5

Candy, chocolate *(cont.)*

milk, with crisps *(Ting-A-Ling)*, 1 oz.	3
milk, with peanuts, 1 oz.	5
semi-sweet	0
cough drops *(Beech-Nut)*	0
cough drops, all flavors *(Pine Bros.)*	0
(Estee-Ets), 5 pieces	< 1
fondant, uncoated	0
fruit and nut mix *(Estee)*, 4 pieces	< 1
fruit flavored *(Bonkers!)*	0
fudge, chocolate, 1 oz.	1
gum, chewing, all varieties	0
gum drops, all flavors	0
hard candy, all flavors	0
(Hot Tamales)	0
jellied candy, all flavors	0
(Jolly Joes)	0
licorice, black or strawberry *(Y&S Twizzlers/ Bites)*	0
lollipop:	
all flavors *(Estee)*	0
all flavors *(Life Savers)*	0
all flavors *(Tootsie Pops)*, 1 oz.	< 1
lozenges, mint	0
marshmallow:	
(Campfire)	0
(Funmallows)	0
(Kraft Jet-Puffed)	0
all shapes *(Rodda)*	0
(Mike & Ike)	0
mint:	
(Andes Creme de Menthe/Mint Parfait), 1 oz.	< 2
(Breath Savers)	0
(Estee)	0

Candy, mint *(cont.)*
    (Kraft Party Mints) 0
    butter *(Kraft)* 0
    peanut *(Andes* Peanut Parfait), 1 oz. . . . . . . < 4
    peanut brittle *(Kraft)* 0
    peanut butter, chocolate coated *(Estee)*,
      1 piece . . . . < 1
    popcorn, plain or flavored, see "Popcorn"
    popcorn, caramel coated:
      (Laura Scudder's) 0
      with peanuts *(Laura Scudder's)* 0
    raisin, chocolate coated *(Estee)*, 6 pieces . . . . < 1
    toffee *(Kraft)* 0
    (Tootsie Roll), 1 oz. . . . . < 1
    wafer *(Necco)* 0

Cannelloni dinner, frozen:
    beef and pork *(Lean Cuisine)*, 9⅝ oz. 50
    cheese *(Lean Cuisine)*, 9⅛ oz. 45

Canola oil, see "Oil"

Cantaloupe:
    fresh 0

Capon, see "Chicken"

Capon giblets, see "Giblets"

Carambola:
    fresh 0

Caraway seeds:
    whole 0

Cardamom seeds:
   whole or ground   0

Cardoon:
   fresh   0

Carissa:
   fresh   0

Carp:
   raw, meat only, 4 oz.   75
   raw, 1 fillet, 7.7 oz. (from 3-lb. whole fish)   143
   baked or broiled, meat only, 4 oz.   95
   baked or broiled, 1 fillet, 6 oz. (7.7 oz. raw) . .   143

Carrot:
   fresh or canned   0
   frozen, without sauce   0

Carrot juice:
   fresh or canned   0

Casaba:
   fresh   0

Cashew:
   raw or roasted   0

Cashew butter:
   raw or toasted   0

Cassava:
   fresh   0

Catfish:

brown bullhead, fresh, raw, meat only, 4 oz. . .   85

channel, raw, meat only, 4 oz.   66

channel, raw, 1 fillet, 2.8 oz. (from 1-lb. whole
fish).   46

Catsup:

bottled   0

Cauliflower:

fresh.   0

frozen, without sauce   0

with almonds, frozen *(Birds Eye)*   0

Cauliflower combinations, frozen:

and green bean festival *(Green Giant Valley
Combination)*   0

and green beans and corn *(Birds Eye)*   0

Caviar:

black and red, granular, 1 oz.   165

black and red, granular, 1 tbsp.   94

Celeriac:

fresh.   0

Celery:

fresh.   0

Celery seed:

whole or ground   0

Celtus:

fresh.   0

Cereal, cooking:

uncooked, regular, quick or instant:

corn (hominy) grits	0
farina	0
oats, oatmeal, or rolled oats	0
oats, maple flavored (*Maypo* Vermont Style)	0
rice	0
wheat	0

Cereal, ready-to-eat, dry:

(*All-Bran*)	0
(*Bran Buds*)	0
bran flakes, 40% and 100% (all brands)	0
(*Cap'n Crunch*)	0
(*Cheerios*)	0
corn flakes (all brands)	0
(*Froot Loops*)	0
(*Golden Grahams*), 1 oz. or about 3/4 cup	tr.
granola (*Nature Valley*)	0
(*Grape-Nuts*)	0
(*Honey Nut Cheerios*)	0
100% "natural," 1 oz.	tr.
(*Product 19*)	0
raisin bran (all brands)	0
(*Rice Krispies*)	0
shredded wheat (all brands)	0
(*Special K*), 1 oz. or about 11/3 cups	tr.
(*Super Sugar Crisp*)	0
(*Sugar Frosted Flakes*)	0
(*Sugar Smacks*)	0
(*Total*)	0
(*Trix*)	0
(*Wheaties*)	0

Cereal beverage mix:
prepared with water 0
prepared with milk, 6 fl. oz. 25
(Postum Regular or Coffee Flavor), prepared
   with water 0

Cervelat, see "Thuringer cervelat"

Champagne, see "Wine"

Chard, Swiss:
fresh 0

Chayote:
fresh 0

Cheddarwurst:
(Hillshire Farm), 1-oz. slice 9

Cheese:
American, processed:
  pasteurized, 1 oz. 27
  pasteurized, 1″ cube 17
  (Kraft Deluxe Loaf or Slices), 1 oz. 25
  (Land O Lakes), 1 oz. 25
  hot pepper *(Sargento),* 1 oz. 27
  pimento, pasteurized, 1 oz. 27
  pimento, pasteurized, 1″ cube 16
  sharp *(Old English* Loaf or Slices), 1 oz. . . . 30
American-Swiss, processed *(Land O Lakes),*
  1 oz. 25
asiago:
  medium *(Universal),* 1 oz. 30
  old *(Universal),* 1 oz. 20

Cheese, asiago *(cont.)*
 soft *(Universal)*, 1 oz.   33
bel dolce, Italian style *(Universal)*, 1 oz.   33
blue:
 1 oz.   21
 crumbled, unpacked, 1 cup   102
 (Dorman's), 1 oz.   21
 (Frigo), 1 oz.   21
 (Kraft), 1 oz.   30
 (Sargento), 1 oz.   21
blue and gorgonzola *(Universal)*, 1 oz.   20
brick:
 1 oz.   27
 1" cube   16
 (Kraft), 1 oz.   30
 (Land O Lakes), 1 oz.   25
 (Sargento), 1 oz.   27
brie, 4 1/2-oz. pkg.   128
brie *(Sargento)*, 1 oz.   28
Camembert:
 1 oz.   20
 1 1/3-oz. wedge   27
 (Sargento), 1 oz.   20
caraway *(Kraft)*, 1 oz.   30
Cheddar:
 1 oz.   30
 shredded, unpacked, 1 cup   119
 (Armour/Armour Lower Salt)*, 1 oz.   30
 (Dorman's), 1 oz.   29
 (Kraft), 1 oz.   30
 (Land O Lakes), 1 oz.   30
 (Sargento), 1 oz.   30
 (Universal), 1 oz.   30
 shredded *(Weight Watchers)*, 1 oz.   28

Cheese *(cont.)*

Cheshire, 1 oz.	29
colby:	
1 oz.	27
1" cube	16
(Armour), 1 oz.	30
(Dorman's), 1 oz.	27
(Kraft), 1 oz.	30
(Land O Lakes), 1 oz.	25
(Sargento), 1 oz.	27
colby jack *(Sargento)*, 1 oz.	27
cottage cheese:	
dry curd, unpacked, 1 cup	10
creamed, unpacked, 1 cup	31
creamed, with fruit, unpacked, 1 cup	25
low fat, 2% fat, unpacked, 1 cup	19
low fat, 2% fat *(Land O Lakes)*, 4 oz.	10
low fat, 1% fat, unpacked, 1 cup	10
(Land O Lakes), 4 oz.	15
cream cheese, regular:	
3-oz. pkg.	93
(Armour Lower Salt), 1 oz.	30
(Philadelphia Brand), 1 oz.	30
with chives or pimentos *(Philadelphia Brand)*,	
1 oz.	30
cream cheese, soft, 1 oz.:	
(Philadelphia Brand)	30
with chives and onion *(Philadelphia Brand)*	30
with peaches, pineapple, or strawberries	
(Philadelphia Brand)	25
cream cheese, whipped, 1 oz.:	
(Philadelphia Brand)	30
with bacon and horseradish *(Philadelphia*	
Brand)	20

Cheese, cream cheese, whipped, 1 oz. *(cont.)*
   with blue cheese *(Philadelphia Brand)* 25
   with chives *(Philadelphia Brand)* 25
   with onions or pimento *(Philadelphia Brand)* 20
   with smoked salmon *(Philadelphia Brand)* . . 25
  Edam:
   7-oz. pkg. 177
   (Dorman's), 1 oz. 25
   (Kraft), 1 oz. 20
   (Land O Lakes), 1 oz. 25
   (Sargento), 1 oz. 25
   (Universal), 1 oz. 25
  farmer's cheese *(Sargento)*, 1 oz. 26
  feta:
   sheep's milk, 1 oz. 25
   (Churny), 1 oz. 25
   (Sargento), 1 oz. 25
  fontina:
   8-oz. pkg. 263
   (Frigo), 1 oz. 33
   (Sargento), 1 oz. 33
  fontinella, Italian, sharp or mild *(Universal)*,
   1 oz. 35
  food, see "Cheese food"
  gjetost *(Ski Queen)*, 1 oz. 20
  Gorgonzola *(Sargento)*, 1 oz. 21
  Gouda:
   7-oz. pkg. 226
   (Kraft), 1 oz. 30
   (Land O Lakes), 1 oz. 30
   (Red Rooster Reduced Sodium), 1 oz. 30
   (Sargento), 1 oz. 32
   (Universal), 1 oz. 32
  Gruyère, 6-oz. pkg. 187

Cheese *(cont.)*

Gruyère *(Sargento)*, 1 oz.	31
havarti *(Casino)*, 1 oz.	35
havarti *(Sargento)*, 1 oz.	31
Italian blend, grated *(Kraft)*, 1 oz.	20
Italian style, grated *(Sargento)*, 1 oz.	26
jalapeño, processed *(Kraft)*, 1 oz.	20
Jarlsberg *(Norseland)*, 1 oz.	16
Jarlsberg *(Sargento)*, 1 oz.	16
limburger:	
8-oz. pkg.	204
(Mohawk Valley Little Gem), 1 oz.	25
(Sargento), 1 oz.	26
Monterey Jack:	
(Armour/Armour Lower Salt), 1 oz.	30
(Kraft), 1 oz.	30
(Sargento), 1 oz.	30
with peppers, jalapeño or mild *(Kraft)*, 1 oz.	30
mozzarella:	
1 oz.	22
(Casino), 1 oz.	25
(Polly-O Lite), 1 oz.	15
(Universal), 1 oz.	25
whole milk *(Frigo)*, 1 oz.	26
whole milk *(Polly-O)*, 1 oz.	20
whole milk *(Sargento)*, 1 oz.	25
part skim *(Frigo)*, 1 oz.	16
part skim *(Kraft)*, 1 oz.	15
part skim *(Land O Lakes)*, 1 oz.	15
part skim *(Polly-O)*, 1 oz.	15
part skim *(Sargento)*, 1 oz.	15
part skim, with jalapeño pepper *(Kraft)*, 1 oz.	20
with pizza spices *(Sargento)*, 1 oz.	15

Cheese *(cont.)*

Muenster:

6-oz. pkg.	163
(Kraft), 1 oz.	30
(Land O Lakes), 1 oz.	25
(Sargento Red Rind), 1 oz.	27
nacho *(Sargento),* 1 oz.	27
Neufchâtel, 3-oz. pkg.	65
Neufchâtel *(Kraft),* 1 oz.	25
Nökkelost *(Norseland),* 1 oz.	26

Parmesan:

hard, 5-oz. pkg.	96
(Frigo), 1 oz.	20
(Kraft Natural), 1 oz.	20
(Sargento), 1 oz.	19
(Universal Loaf), 1 oz.	19
grated, 1 tbsp.	4
grated *(Frigo),* 1 oz.	23
grated *(Kraft),* 1 oz.	30
grated *(Sargento),* 1 oz.	22
grated *(Universal),* 1 oz.	25
Parmesan and Romano, grated *(Frigo),* 1 oz.	28
Parmesan and Romano, grated *(Sargento),* 1 oz.	24
pimento, processed *(Kraft Deluxe),* 1 oz.	25
Port du Salut, 1 oz.	35

provolone:

6-oz. pkg.	117
(Dorman's), 1 oz.	19
(Kraft), 1 oz.	25
(Land O Lakes), 1 oz.	20
(Sargento), 1 oz.	20
(Universal, Half Moon, Stick or Slices), 1 oz.	25

Cheese *(cont.)*

queso blanco *(Sargento)*, 1 oz.	27
queso de papa *(Sargento)*, 1 oz.	30
ricotta:	
whole milk, 1 cup	124
whole milk *(Frigo)*, 1 oz.	15
whole milk *(Sargento)*, 1 oz.	15
whole milk and whey *(Sargento)*, 1 oz.	13
part skim, 1 cup	76
part skim *(Frigo)*, 1 oz.	10
part skim *(Polly-O)*, 1 oz.	10
part skim *(Sargento)*, 1 oz.	10
Romano:	
5-oz. pkg.	148
(Casino Natural), 1 oz.	30
(Frigo), 1 oz.	30
(Sargento), 1 oz.	29
(Universal Loaf), 1 oz.	21
grated *(Frigo)*, 1 oz.	35
grated *(Kraft)*, 1 oz.	30
grated *(Universal)*, 1 oz.	25
Roquefort, 3-oz. pkg.	76
Roquefort, 1 oz.	26
scamorze, part skim *(Kraft)*, 1 oz.	15
smoked *(Sargento Smokestik)*, 1 oz.	24
spread, see "Cheese spreads"	
string cheese, regular or smoked *(Sargento)*, 1 oz.	15
Swiss, natural:	
1 oz.	26
1" cube	14
(Dorman's), 1 oz.	24
(Kraft), 1 oz.	25

Cheese, Swiss, natural *(cont.)*
  (Land O Lakes), 1 oz.   25
  (Sargento), 1 oz.   26
  aged *(Kraft)*, 1 oz.   26
  Swiss, processed:
  pasteurized, 1 oz.   24
  pasteurized, 1" cube   15
  (Kraft Deluxe), 1 oz.   25
  taco cheese *(Sargento)*, 1 oz.   27
  taco cheese, shredded *(Kraft)*, 1 oz.   30
  tilsit, whole milk, 1 oz.   29
  tilsiter *(Sargento)*, 1 oz.   29
  tybo *(Sargento* Red Wax), 1 oz.   23
  (Weight Watchers Chunks or Sticks), 1 oz. . . .   28
  (Weight Watchers Slices), 1 oz.   8

Cheese, imitation:
  American *(Sandwich-Mate)*, 1 oz. . . . .   < 5
  Cheddar:
    (Ched-O-Mate), 1 oz.   5
    (Frigo), 1 oz.   0
    (Sargento), 1 oz.   2
    mild *(Golden Image)*, 1 oz.   5
  (Cheez-Ola/Cheez-Ola Reduced Sodium), 1 oz.
    . . . .   < 5
  (Chef's Delight), 1 oz. . . . .   < 5
  colby *(Golden Image)*, 1 oz.   5
  (Count Down), 1 oz. . . . .   < 5
  mozzarella:
    (Frigo), 1 oz.   0
    (Pizza-Mate), 1 oz. . . . .   < 5
    (Sargento), 1 oz.   2
  Parmesan *(Sargento)*, 1 oz.   3
  semi-soft *(Dorman's)*, 1 oz.   4

Cheese, spreads:
American, pasteurized process:

5-oz. jar	78
(Kraft), 1 oz.	20
(Sargento Sharp or Pimento), 1 oz.	27
and bacon *(Kraft),* 1 oz.	20
and bacon *(Squeez-A-Snak),* 1 oz.	20
blue *(Roka Brand),* 1 oz.	20
brick *(Sargento),* 1 oz.	25
(Cheez Whiz), 1 oz.	20
cream cheese, see "Cheese"	
with garlic *(Kraft),* 1 oz.	15
garlic or hickory smoke flavor *(Squeez-A-Snak),*	
1 oz.	20
with jalapeño peppers *(Cheez Whiz),* 1 oz. . . .	15
jalapeño pepper *(Kraft),* 1 oz.	15
(Land O Lakes Golden Velvet), 1 oz.	15
limburger *(Mohawk Valley),* 1 oz.	20
Mexican, hot or mild *(Velveeta),* 1 oz.	20
olive and pimento *(Kraft),* 1 oz.	15
pimento:	
(Cheez Whiz), 1 oz.	15
(Kraft), 1 oz.	15
(Squeez-A-Snak), 1 oz.	20
(Velveeta), 1 oz.	20
pineapple or relish *(Kraft),* 1 oz.	15
relish *(Kraft)*	70
sharp:	
(Old English), 1 oz.	20
(Squeez-A-Snak), 1 oz.	20
(Velveeta), 1 oz.	20
Swiss *(Sargento),* 1 oz.	24
(Velveeta Loaf or Slices), 1 oz.	20

Cheese and bacon dip:
  (Nalley's), 1 oz. 33

Cheese dip, see specific listings

Cheese food:
  American:
    cold pack, pasteurized process, 1 oz. 18
    (Dorman's), 1 oz. 6
    (Golden Image), 1 oz. 5
    (Kraft Singles), 1 oz. 20
    (Sargento Burger Cheese), 1 oz. 27
    grated *(Kraft)*, 1 oz. 10
    product *(Harvest Moon Brand)*, 1 oz. 15
    product *(Light n' Lively)*, 1 oz. 15
   with bacon:
    (Cheez 'n Bacon Singles), 1 oz. 20
    (Cracker Barrel), 1 oz. 20
    (Kraft), 1 oz. 20
   Cheddar:
    (Land O Lakes LaChedda), 1 oz. 20
    (Light n' Lively), 1 oz. 15
    cold pack *(Kaukauna)*, 1 oz. 25
    Port wine *(Cracker Barrel)*, 1 oz. 20
    sharp or extra sharp *(Cracker Barrel)*, 1 oz. 20
   with garlic *(Kraft)*, 1 oz. 20
   jalapeño *(Kraft* Singles), 1 oz. 25
   jalapeño *(Land O Lakes)*, 1 oz. 20
   Monterey Jack *(Kraft* Singles), 1 oz. 25
   onion *(Land O Lakes)*, 1 oz. 15
   pepperoni *(Land O Lakes)*, 1 oz. 20
   pimento *(Kraft* Singles), 1 oz. 20
   product *(Harvest Moon Brand)*, 1 oz. 15
   salami *(Land O Lakes)*, 1 oz. 20

Cheese food *(cont.)*
sharp *(Kraft Singles)*, 1 oz. 25
smoked *(Smokelle)*, 1 oz. 20
Swiss:
  pasteurized process, 1 oz. 23
  (Kraft Singles), 1 oz. 25
  (Light n' Lively), 1 oz. 15

Cheese-nut balls or logs:
Cheddar with almonds *(Sargento)*, 1 oz. 18
Port wine with almonds *(Cracker Barrel)*, 1 oz. 15
Port wine with almonds *(Sargento)*, 1 oz. 18
sharp or smoky with almonds *(Cracker Barrel)*,
  1 oz. 15
Swiss with almonds *(Sargento)*, 1 oz. 21

Cheese sauce mix:
dehydrated, 1.2-oz. packet 18
dehydrated, prepared with milk, 1 cup 53

Cherimoya:
fresh 0

Cherries:
sour or sweet, fresh, canned, or frozen 0

Cherry, maraschino:
canned or in jars 0

Cherry drink:
canned or mix 0

Cherry roll or bar:
natural or sweetened 0

Chervil:
fresh or dried   0

Chestnut:
European or Oriental, raw, dried, steamed, or
roasted   0

Chestnut flour:
4 oz.   0

Chewing gum, see "Candy"

Chick peas:
raw, dried, or canned   0
marinated, canned *(S&W)*, 1 cup   0

Chicken, edible portions:
broilers or fryers, raw:
meat and skin, 9.7 oz. (yield per 1 lb. with
bone)   208
broilers or fryers, fried* :
meat and skin, 6.6 oz. (yield per 1 lb. raw
with bone)   169
meat and skin, 1/2 chicken (15.6 oz. with
bone)   283
meat only, 4 oz.   107
meat only, chopped or diced, 1 cup or 4.9
oz.   131
dark meat only, 4 oz.   109
light meat only, 4 oz.   102
skin only, 1 oz.   21

* *Flour-coated; fried in vegetable shortening*

Chicken, broilers or fryers, fried *(cont.)*

    breast, with skin, 1/2 breast (4.2 oz. with
        bone)   88

    breast, meat only, 1/2 breast   78

    drumstick, with skin, 1 drumstick (2.6 oz. with
        bone)   44

    drumstick, meat only, 1 drumstick   40

    leg, with skin, 1 leg (5.5 oz. with bone) 105

    leg, meat only, 1 leg   93

    thigh, with skin, 1 thigh (2.9 oz. with bone)   60

    thigh, meat only, 1 thigh   53

    wing, with skin, 1 wing (2.2 oz. with bone) . .   39

    wing, meat only, 1 wing   17

  broilers or fryers, roasted:

    meat and skin, 6.3 oz. (yield per 1 lb. raw
        with bone) 157

    meat and skin, 1/2 chicken (15.8 oz. with
        bone) 263

    meat only, 4 oz. 101

    meat only, chopped or diced, 1 cup or 4.9
        oz. 125

    dark meat only, 4 oz. 105

    light meat only, 4 oz.   96

    skin only, 1 oz.   24

    breast, with skin, 1/2 breast (4.2 oz. with
        bone)   83

    drumstick, with skin, 1 drumstick (2.9 oz. with
        bone)   48

    leg, with skin, 1 leg (5.7 oz. with bone) 105

    thigh, with skin, 1 thigh (2.9 oz. with bone)   58

    wing, with skin, 1 wing (2.3 oz. with bone) . .   29

  broilers or fryers, stewed or simmered:

    meat and skin, 7.1 oz. (yield per 1 lb. raw
        with bone) 157

Chicken, broilers or fryers, stewed or simmered *(cont.)*
  meat and skin, 1/2 chicken (1.1 lbs. with
    bone)   262
  meat only, 4 oz.   94
  meat only, chopped or diced, 1 cup or 4.9
    oz.   116
  dark meat only, 4 oz.   100
  light meat only, 4 oz.   87
  breast, with skin, 1/2 breast (4.8 oz. with
    bone)   83
  breast, meat only, 1/2 breast   73
  drumstick, with skin, 1 drumstick (3.1 oz. with
    bone)   48
  drumstick, meat only, 1 drumstick.   40
  leg, with skin, 1 leg (6.3 oz. with bone)   105
  leg, meat only, 1 leg   90
  thigh, with skin, 1 thigh (3.2 oz. with bone)   57
  thigh, meat only, 1 thigh   49
  wing, with skin, 1 wing (2.7 oz. with bone) . .   28
  wing, meat only, 1 wing   18
  capon, raw:
    meat and skin, 10.5 oz. (yield per 1 lb. with
      bone)   222
  capon, roasted:
    meat and skin, 6.9 oz. (yield per 1 lb. raw
      with bone)   169
    meat and skin, 1/2 capon (2 lbs. with bone)   549
    meat and skin, 4 oz.   98
  giblets, see "Giblets"
  roasters, raw:
    meat and skin, 10.3 oz. (yield per 1 lb. with
      bone)   212
  roasters, roasted:
    meat and skin, 7.4 oz. (yield per 1 lb. raw
      with bone)   136

Chicken, roasters, roasted *(cont.)*

    meat and skin, 1/2 chicken (1.5 lbs. with
bone) 365

    meat only, dark or light, 4 oz. 85

    dark meat only, chopped or diced, 1 cup or
4.9 oz. 104

    light meat only, chopped or diced, 1 cup or
4.9 oz. 105

  stewing, raw:

    meat and skin, 9.6 oz. (yield per 1 lb. with
bone) 192

  stewing, stewed or simmered:

    meat and skin, 6.3 oz. (yield per 1 lb. raw
with bone) 140

    meat and skin, 1/2 chicken (13.5 oz. with
bone) 205

    meat only, 4 oz. 94

    meat only, chopped or diced, 1 cup or
4.9 oz. 117

    dark meat only, 4 oz. 108

    dark meat only, chopped or diced, 1 cup or
4.9 oz. 132

    light meat only, 4 oz. 79

    light meat only, chopped or diced, 1 cup or
4.9 oz. 98

Chicken, sliced and luncheon meat:

  breast *(Oscar Mayer),* 1-oz. slice 11

  breast, oven-roasted *(Louis Rich),* 1-oz. slice 14

  roll, light meat, 6-oz. pkg. 85

  roll, light meat, 2 oz. 28

  smoked *(Carl Buddig),* 1 oz. 15

Chicken chow mein, frozen, see "Chicken
dinner," and "Chicken entrée, frozen"

Chicken chow mein entrée, canned:

drained *(Chun King* Divider Pak/4 Servings), 7.14 oz.	13
drained *(Chun King* Divider Pak/2 Servings), 8.11 oz.	11
(Chun King Stir-Fry), 6 oz. with chicken	44

Chicken dinner, frozen:

à la orange *(Lean Cuisine)*, 8 oz.	45
and vegetables *(Lean Cuisine)*, 12¾ oz.	40
breast, medallions Marsala *(Classic Lite)*, 11 oz.	85
breast, roast *(Classic Lite)*, 11 oz.	85
Burgundy *(Classic Lite)*, 11¼ oz.	70
cacciatore *(Lean Cuisine)*, 10⅞ oz.	40
chow mein *(Classic Lite)*, 10½ oz.	60
chow mein *(Lean Cuisine)*, 11¼ oz.	25
fricassee *(Dinner Classics)*, 11¾ oz.	75
glazed *(Lean Cuisine)*, 8½ oz.	55
Oriental *(Classic Lite)*, 10½ oz.	65
sweet and sour *(Classic Lite)*, 11 oz.	70
sweet and sour *(Dinner Classics)*, 11 oz.	65
teriyaki *(Dinner Classics)*, 10½ oz.	70

Chicken entrée, frozen:

chow mein *(Chun King* Boil-in-Bag), 10 oz.	28
cordon bleu *(Beatrice* International Entrees), 6 oz.	85
Kiev *(Beatrice* International Entrees), 6 oz.	105
Lucerne *(Beatrice* International Entrees), 6 oz.	50
Oriental *(Chun King* Boil-in-Bag), 10 oz.	26
Parmigiana *(Beatrice* International Entrees), 6 oz.	50
Romanoff *(Beatrice* International Entrees), 6 oz.	55

Chicken entrée *(cont.)*
  royale *(Beatrice* International Entrees), 6 oz. . . 50
  sweet and sour *(Chun King* Boil-in-Bag), 10 oz. 26
  walnut chicken, chunky *(Chun King* Boil-in-
    Bag), 10 oz. 31

Chicken and fish seasoning:
  (Lawry's Natural Choice for Chicken and Fish) 0

Chicken frankfurter:
  1 oz. 28
  1.6-oz. link 45

Chicken giblets, see "Giblets"

Chicken gizzard, see "Gizzard"

Chicken gravy:
  canned, 10 1/2-oz. can 6
  canned, 1 cup 5
  dehydrated mix, .8-oz. packet 2

Chicken heart, see "Heart"

Chicken liver, see "Liver"

Chicken, smoked, see "Chicken, sliced and
  luncheon meat"

Chicken-turkey spread, see "Poultry salad"

Chicory, witloof, see "Endive, French or
  Belgian"

Chicory greens:
fresh   0

Chicory root:
fresh or dried   0

Chili con carne:
with beans, canned, 1/2 cup   22
without beans, canned:
   (Nalley's), 31/2 oz.   20
   (Nalley's Big Chunk), 31/2 oz.   30
   mild, hot, or thick *(Nalley's)* 31/2 oz.   15

Chili con carne spread:
concentrate *(Oscar Mayer),* 1 oz.   14

Chili pepper, see "Pepper, chili"

Chili powder:
seasoned, mild or hot   0

Chili sauce:
meatless, canned or bottled   0

Chitterlings, see "Pork chitterlings"

Chives:
fresh or freeze-dried   0

Chocolate, see "Candy"

Chocolate, baking:
milk, 1 oz.   6
dark or sweet   0

Chocolate, baking *(cont.)*
  semi-sweet   0

Chocolate milk, see "Milk, chocolate, dairy" and
  "Milk, chocolate, mix"

Chocolate sauce, see "Toppings, dessert"

Chocolate syrup:
  (Nestlé Quik Syrup)   0
  (Smucker's)   0

Chow mein, see specific listings

Chrysanthemum garland:
  fresh   0

Cinnamon:
  whole or ground   0

Cisco:
  smoked, meat only, 4 oz.   36

Citron:
  candied   0

Citrus juice or drink:
  canned, frozen, or mix   0

Clam:
  hardshell, fresh, raw, meat only, 4 oz.   35
  mixed species:
    raw, in shell, 9 large or 20 small   60
    raw, meat only, 4 oz.   39

Clam, mixed species *(cont.)*

    steamed or poached, 20 small 60

    steamed or poached, meat only, 4 oz. 76

    canned, drained, 4 oz. 76

    canned, drained, 1 cup 107

Clam chowder, see "Soup"

Clam dip:

    (Kraft), 2 tbsp. 10

    (Kraft Premium), 1 oz. 20

    (Nalley's), 1 oz. 11

Cloves:

    whole or ground 0

Coating mix, see "Seasoned coating mix"

Cocktail, alcoholic, see specific listings

Cocktail drink mix:

    (Bar-Tender's), prepared with alcohol 0

Cocktail sauce:

    (Dia-Mel) 0

    (Sauceworks) 0

Cocoa:

    powder, with non-fat dry milk, 1 oz. 1

    powder, without non-fat dry milk 0

    powder *(Alba),* .7 oz. 4

Cocoa oil, see "Oil"

Coconut:
  fresh or canned 0

Coconut cream or milk:
  fresh or canned 0

Coconut oil, see "Oil"

Cod:
  Atlantic, fresh:
    raw, meat only, 4 oz. 49
    raw, 1 fillet, 8.1 oz. (from 3-lb. whole fish) . . 99
    baked or broiled, meat only, 4 oz. 62
    baked or broiled, 1 fillet, 6.3 oz. (8.1 oz. raw) 99
  Atlantic, canned:
    with liquid, 11-oz. can 171
    with liquid, 4 oz. 62
  Atlantic, dried and salted, meat only, 2 oz. . . . 86
  Pacific, fresh:
    raw, meat only, 4 oz. 42
    raw, 1 fillet, 4.1 oz. (from 1½-lb. whole fish) 43

Cod, ling, see "Lingcod"

Cod dinner, frozen:
  almondine *(Dinner Classics),* 12 oz. 75

Cod-liver oil:
  1 oz. 162

Coffee:
  plain, regular, instant, or freeze-dried 0

Coffee liqueur:
  all varieties, uncreamed 0

Coffee substitute, see "Cereal beverage mix"

Coffee whitener, see "Cream, imitation"

Cognac, see "Liquor"

Colada drink mixer:
piña *(Freeze & Serve)*   0
piña, bottled *(Coco Casa)*, 1 fl. oz.   88
piña, dry or bottled *(Holland-House)*   0
piña, mix* *(Bar-Tender's)*, 5 fl. oz.   12

Collard greens:
fresh   0
frozen, without sauce   0

Collins drink mix:
(Bar-Tender's), prepared with alcohol   0

Conch:
fresh, raw, meat only, 4 oz.   160

Cookie:
animal crackers *(Sunshine)*   0
brownie, with nuts, frosted, 1 piece, .9 oz. . . .   14
butter flavor *(Orbit)*   0
butter flavor *(Sunshine)*   0
chocolate *(Orbit)*   0
chocolate chip:
  (Chip-A-Roos)   0
  (Sunshine Nuggets)   0
  butterscotch *(Chippy Chews)*   0

_____
* Prepared according to package directions

Cookie, chocolate chip *(cont.)*

chocolate *(Chip-A-Roos)*	0
fudge *(Chippy Chews)*	0
peanut butter *(Chippy Chews)*	0
raisin *(Chippy Chews)*	0
chocolate sandwich *(Tru Blu)*	0
creme sandwich:	
chocolate or vanilla	0
(Frito-Lay's Duplex), 2 1/2 oz.	5
(Hydrox)	0
(Vienna Fingers)	0
custard sandwich *(Sunshine Cup Custard)*	0
fig bar, 1 piece, 1 5/8″ square × 3/8″	7
fig bar *(Sunshine Fig Chewies)*	0
fudge sandwich *(Chips 'n Middles)*	0
fudge sandwich *(Sunshine)*	0
ginger snaps *(Sunshine)*	0
graham crackers, regular, honey or cinnamon	0
lemon:	
(Sunshine Lemon Coolers)	0
sandwich *(Tru Blu)*	0
marshmallow *(Mallo Puffs)*	0
molasses *(Grandma's* Old Time), 3 oz.	10
oatmeal:	
(Sunshine Country Style)	0
apple spice *(Grandma's)*, 3 oz.	10
peanut sandwich *(Sunshine)*	0
with raisins, 1 piece, 2 5/8″ diam. × 1/4″	< 1
peanut butter:	
(Sunshine Wafers)	0
sandwich *(Chips 'n Middles)*	0
raisin:	
(Grandma's Soft), 3 oz.	10
(Sunshine Golden Fruit)	0

Cookie *(cont.)*
shortbread, 4 pieces, 1.4 oz.   27
sprinkled *(Sunshine Sprinkles)*   0
sugar wafers *(Sunshine)*   0
toy cookies *(Sunshine)*   0
vanilla sandwich *(Tru Blu)*   0
vanilla wafers, 10 pieces, 1¾" diam. × ¼" . .   25
vanilla wafers *(Sunshine)*, 4 pieces   5

Cookie dough, refrigerated:
chocolate chip, baked, 4 pieces, 2¼" diam. ×
⅜"   22
sugar, baked, 4 pieces, 2½" diam. × ¼" . . .   29

Cookie mix*:
brownie *(Estee)*, 2" × 2" piece   30

Coriander:
fresh or dried   0

Coriander seed:
whole or ground   0

Corn:
white or yellow, fresh   0
canned or frozen, whole kernel or cream style   0

Corn, green beans, and pasta curls:
frozen *(Birds Eye)*, 3.3 oz.   0

Corn chips:
regular, barbecue or onion flavored   0

---
* Prepared according to package directions

Corn chips *(cont.)*
  cheese flavored:
    (Chee.Tos Regular, Balls or Rods), 1 oz. . . .   tr.
    (Jax Regular or Crunchy)   0
    Cheddar *(Chee.Tos/Chee.Tos Cheddar*
      Valley), 1 oz. . . . .   tr.
  chili cheese flavored *(Fritos),* 1 oz. . . . .   tr.

Corn grits:
  white or yellow, dry   0
  with imitation bacon or ham bits, dry *(Quaker)*   0
  canned, white or yellow, plain or with pepper   0

Corn meal:
  white or yellow, dry   0

Corn oil, see "Oil"

Corn salad:
  fresh, whole   0

Corn syrup:
  dark or light *(Karo)*   0

Corned beef, see "Beef, corned"

Cornstarch:
  (Argo/Kingsford's)   0

Cough drops, see "Candy"

Cotto salami, see "Salami"

Cottonseed flour:
partially defatted or lowfat 0

Cottonseed kernels:
roasted 0

Cottonseed meal:
partially defatted 0

Cottonseed oil, see "Oil"

Couscous mix:
pilaf, dry *(Casbah)* 0

Cowpeas:
raw or canned, plain 0
canned, with pork, 1 cup 17

Cowpeas, leafy-tips:
fresh 0

Crab:
Alaska king:
  raw, meat only, 4 oz. 48
  raw, meat only, 1 leg or 6.1 oz. (from 1-lb.
    whole leg) 72
  steamed or poached, meat only, 4 oz. 60
  steamed or poached, meat only, 1 leg or
    4.7 oz. 72
blue, fresh:
  raw, meat only, 4 oz. 88
  raw, meat only, 3/4 oz. (from 5.3-oz. whole
    crab) 16
  steamed or poached, meat only, 4 oz. 113

Crab, blue, fresh *(cont.)*
    steam or poached, meat only, 1 cup or
        4.8 oz. 135
    blue, canned:
    drained or dry pack, 4 oz. 101
    drained or dry pack, 1 cup 120
    Dungeness:
    raw, meat only, 4 oz. 70
    raw, meat only, 5.7 oz. (from 1½-lb. whole
        crab) 97
    queen, raw, meat only, 4 oz. 62

Crab, imitation:
    Alaska king, made from surimi, meat only, 4 oz. 23

Crabapple:
    fresh 0

Cracker:
    butter flavor *(Hi-Ho)* 0
    and cheese *(Handi-Snacks)*, 1 pkg. 15
    cheese:
        10 pieces, 1″ square 6
        (Cheez-It) 0
        Cheddar *(American Heritage)*, 5 pieces 5
        Parmesan *(American Heritage)* 0
    garlic *(Manischewitz Garlic Tams)* 0
    graham crackers, see "Cookies"
    (Kavli Norwegian Thick or Thin) 0
    (Manischewitz Tam Tam) 0
    matzo:
        (Manischewitz Passover/Unsalted) 0
        egg *(Manischewitz Passover)*, 10 pieces . . . 20
        egg *(Manischewitz Passover)*, 1.2-oz. piece 25

Cracker, matzo *(cont.)*

egg and onion *(Manischewitz)*, 1-oz. piece . .	15
miniature *(Manischewitz)*	0
tea, thin *(Manischewitz)*	0
thins, diatetic *(Manischewitz)*	0
wheat *(Manischewitz)*	0
whole wheat with bran *(Manischewitz)*	0
melba toast, plain	0
onion *(Manischewitz Onion Tams)*	0
oyster and soup *(Sunshine)*	0
peanut butter and cheese sandwich, 1 piece, .3 oz.	1
peanut butter and cheese sandwich *(Handi-Snacks)*	0
rye wafers, whole-grain	0
rye bran *(Kavli)*	0
saltines:	
made with lard, .4 oz. or 4 pieces	4
(Krispy)	0
(Premium)	0
(Zesta)	0
sesame *(American Heritage)*	0
soda or snack	0
(Sunshine Cafe Crackers)	0
wheat:	
(American Heritage)	0
(Manischewitz Wheat Tams)	0
(Sunshine Wafers)	0
thins	0
whole wheat wafers	0

Cracker crumbs and meal:

cracker *(Nabisco)*	0
matzo *(Manischewitz Farfel)*	0

Cracker crumbs and meal *(cont.)*
　matzo meal *(Manischewitz)* . . . .　0

Cranberries:
　fresh, canned, or frozen . . . .　0

Cranberry juice or drink:
　plain or mixed fruit, canned, bottled, or frozen　0

Cranberry-orange relish:
　fresh or in jars . . . .　0

Cranberry sauce:
　whole or jellied, canned . . . .　0

Crayfish:
　raw, meat only, 8 crayfish or 1 oz. (15–25 per
　　lb. whole) . . . .　37
　raw, meat only, 4 oz. . . . .　158
　steamed or poached, meat only, 4 oz. . . . . . .　202

Cream:
　half and half:
　　1 cup . . . .　89
　　1 tbsp. . . . .　6
　heavy, whipping:
　　unwhipped, 1 cup . . . .　326
　　unwhipped, 1 tbsp. . . . .　21
　　whipped, 1 cup . . . .　163
　　whipped, 1 tbsp. . . . .　11
　light, coffee or table:
　　1 cup . . . .　159
　　1 tbsp. . . . .　10

Cream *(cont.)*
  light, whipping:
    unwhipped, 1 cup   265
    unwhipped, 1 tbsp.   17
    whipped, 1 cup   133
    whipped, 1 tbsp.   9
  medium, 25% fat:
    1 cup   209
    1 tbsp.   17
  sour:
    1 cup   102
    1 tbsp.   5
  sour, half and half, 1 tbsp.   6
  whipped, topping:
    pressurized, 1 cup   46
    pressurized, 1 tbsp.   2
    frozen *(Kraft* Real Cream), 1/4 cup   10

Cream, imitation (non-dairy):
  regular or sour, dry, liquid, or frozen   0
  whipping, unwhipped, prewhipped, or
    pressurized   0
  whipped topping, pressurized, semi-solid, or
    mix   0

Cream puff, frozen:
  Bavarian or chocolate *(Rich's),* 1 puff   35

Crème de menthe liqueur:
  green or white   0

Cress, garden:
  fresh.   0

Cress, water, see "Watercress"

Croaker:
  Atlantic, raw:
    meat only, 4 oz. 69
    1 fillet, 2.8 oz. (from 1-lb. whole fish) 48

Croissant:
  2-oz. piece 13

Crowder peas:
  fresh or frozen 0

Cucumber:
  fresh 0

Cumin seed:
  whole or ground 0

Cupcake, see "Cake, snack"

Cupu assu, see "Oil"

Currant:
  black, red, or white, fresh or dried 0

Curry powder:
  mild or hot 0

Curry sauce:
  dry mix, 1.2-oz. packet . . . . tr.
  dry mix, prepared with milk, 1 cup 35

Cusk:
  raw, meat only, 4 oz.   46
  raw, 1 fillet, 4.3 oz. (from 2-lb. whole fish)   50

Custard, see "Pudding, ready-to-serve"

Cuttlefish:
  raw, meat only, 4 oz.   127

D

Daiquiri cocktail:

fluid or mix 0

Dairy Queen/Brazier:

sandwiches, 1 piece:

  chicken, 7.9 oz. 75

  fish, 6 oz. 50

  fish, with cheese, 6.3 oz. 60

  hamburger:

    single, 5.3 oz. 45

    double, 7.5 oz. 85

    triple, 9.7 oz. 135

  hamburger with cheese:

    single, 5.8 oz. 50

    double, 8.5 oz. 95

    triple, 10.8 oz. 145

Dairy Queen/Brazier, sandwiches *(cont.)*

   hot dog:

      plain, 3.5 oz. 45

      with cheese, 4 oz. 55

      with chili, 4.6 oz. 55

   hot dog, super:

      plain, 6.3 oz. 80

      with cheese, 7 oz. 100

      with chili, 7.8 oz. 100

  side dishes, 1 serving:

   French fries, regular, 2.5 oz. 10

   French fries, large, 4 oz. 15

   onion rings, 3 oz. 15

  desserts and shakes, 1 serving:

   banana split, 13.7 oz. 30

   Buster Bar, 5.3 oz. 10

   cone, small, 3 oz. 10

   cone, regular, 5.1 oz. 15

   cone, large, 7.6 oz. 25

   cone, dipped, chocolate, small, 3.3 oz. 10

   cone, dipped, chocolate, regular, 5.6 oz. . . . 20

   cone, dipped, chocolate, large, 8.4 oz. 30

   Dairy Queen frozen dessert, 4 oz. 15

   Dilly bar, 3 oz. 10

   Double Delight, 9.1 oz. 25

   DQ sandwich, 2.1 oz. 5

   float, 14.2 oz. 20

   freeze, 14.2 oz. 30

   hot fudge *Brownie Delight,* 9.5 oz. 20

   malt, chocolate, small, 10.4 oz. 35

   malt, chocolate, regular, 14.9 oz. 50

   malt, chocolate, large, 21 oz. 70

   Mr. Misty, all sizes 0

Dairy Queen/Brazier, desserts and shakes *(cont.)*

Mr. Misty float, 14.7 oz.	20
Mr. Misty freeze, 14.7 oz.	30
Mr. Misty Kiss, 3.2 oz.	0
parfait, 10.1 oz.	30
Peanut Butter Parfait, 10.9 oz.	30
shake, chocolate, small, 10.4 oz.	35
shake, chocolate, regular, 14.9 oz.	50
shake, chocolate, large, 21 oz.	70
strawberry shortcake, 11.4 oz.	25
sundae, chocolate, small, 3.8 oz.	10
sundae, chocolate, regular, 6.3 oz.	20
sundae, chocolate, large, 8.8 oz.	30

Dandelion greens:

fresh	0

Danish pastry, see specific listings

Date:

domestic or imported, natural or dry	0

Date, Chinese, see "Jujube"

Dill pickle dip:

(Nalley's), 1 oz.	11

Dip (see also specific listings):

flavored *(Land O Lakes),* 2 oz.	10
mix* *(Estee),* 2 tbsp.	16

---
* Prepared according to package directions

Dock:
  fresh   0

Dolphin fish:
  fresh, raw, meat only, 4 oz.   83
  fresh, raw, 1 fillet, 7.2 oz. (from 3-lb. whole
    fish)   149

Dogfish, see "Shark"

Domino's Pizza:
  cheese, 2 slices or 1/4 of 12" pie   10
  cheese, 2 slices or 1/6 of 16" pie   40
  pepperoni, 2 slices or 1/4 of 12" pie   30
  pepperoni, 2 slices or 1/6 of 16" pie   60

Doughnut:
  cinnamon *(Hostess),* 1 piece   6
  chocolate coated *(Hostess),* 1 piece   4
  chocolate coated, mini *(Hostess Donettes),* 1
    piece   4
  krunch *(Hostess),* 1 piece   4
  old-fashioned *(Hostess),* 1 piece   9
  old-fashioned, glazed *(Hostess),* 1 piece   11
  plain *(Hostess),* 1 piece   7
  powdered sugar *(Hostess),* 1 piece   6
  powdered sugar, mini *(Hostess Donettes),* 1
    piece   2

Drum:
  freshwater:
    raw, meat only, 4 oz.   73
    raw, 7-oz. fillet (from 2 1/2-lb. whole fish) . . .   127

Duck, edible portions:
  domestic, raw:
    meat and skin, 10.1 oz. (yield per 1 lb. with
      bone)   218
  domestic, roasted:
    meat and skin, 6.1 oz. (yield per 1 lb. raw
      with bone)   145
    meat and skin, 1/2 duck (1.3 lbs. with bone)   320
    meat only, 4 oz.   101
  wild, raw:
    meat and skin, 8.4 oz. (yield per 1 lb. with
      bone)   191
    meat and skin, 1/2 duck (15.9 oz. with bone)   216
    breast meat only, 4 oz.   140

Duck fat:
  raw, 1 oz.   28

Duck liver, see "Liver"

Dutch brand loaf:
  pork and beef, 1-oz. slice   68

E

meat, baked or broiled

Food and Measure	Cholesterol (mgs.)
Eclair:	
chocolate, frozen *(Rich's)*, 1 piece	35
Eel:	
European, fresh, meat only, 4 oz.	122
mixed species, fresh:	
raw, meat only, 4 oz.	143
raw, 1 fillet, 7.2 oz. (from 2-lb. whole fish) . .	257
baked or broiled, meat only, 4 oz.	183
baked or broiled, 1 fillet, 5.6 oz. (7.2 oz. raw)	257
Egg:	
chicken, fresh, raw:	
jumbo *(A&P Quality)*, 1 egg	340
extra large *(A&P Grade A)*, 1 egg	305
large, 1 egg	274

Egg, chicken, fresh, raw *(cont.)*

large, white of 1 egg	0
large, yolk of 1 egg	272
medium *(A&P* Grade A), 1 egg.	235
small *(A&P* Grade A), 1 egg	205
chicken, fresh, boiled or poached, large, 1 egg	274

chicken, dried:

whole, 1 oz.	544
whole, 1/2 cup sifted	816
whole, 1 tbsp.	96
white, flakes or powder, stabilized, 1 oz. . . .	0
yolk, 1 oz.	830
yolk, 1 tbsp.	117
duck, fresh, raw, whole, 1 average egg	619
quail, fresh, raw, whole, 1 average egg	76
turkey, fresh, raw, whole, 1 average egg	737

Egg, substitute:

frozen, 1 cup	5
liquid, 1 cup	3
powder, 1 cup	113
(Fleischmann's Egg Beaters)	0
99% real egg, with cheese	
(Fleischmann's Egg Beaters), 1/2 cup	5

Egg foo yung:

canned *(Chun-King* Stir Fry), 5 oz.*	142

Egg roll, frozen:

chicken *(Chun King)*, .65-oz. roll with sauce**	2
meat-shrimp *(Chun King)*, .65-oz. roll with sauce**	4

---

* *Prepared according to package directions*
** *Mustard packet, prepared with water*

Egg roll *(cont.)*
  meat-shrimp *(Chun King)*, 2.6-oz. roll with
    sauce* 14
  shrimp *(Chun King)*, .65-oz. roll with sauce* . . 3

Eggnog:
  1 cup 149
  1 quart 596
  (Flav-O-Rich), 8 fl. oz. 135
  (Land O Lakes), 8 fl. oz. 123

Eggnog flavor mix:
  prepared with milk, 1 cup 33

Eggplant:
  fresh 0

Elderberries:
  fresh 0

Enchilada dip:
  (Fritos), 3 1/8 oz. 5

Enchilada sauce:
  canned, hot or mild *(Del Monte* Cooking
    Sauce) 0

Endive, curly:
  fresh 0

Endive, French or Belgian:
  fresh 0

Escarole, see "Endive, curly"

---

* *Mustard packet, prepared with water*

F

Food and Measure	Cholesterol (mgs.)

Falafel mix:
  dry *(Casbah)* 0

Fat, see specific listings

Fat substitute:
  (Rokeach Neutral Nyafat) 0

Fennel leaves:
  fresh 0

Fennel seed:
  whole or ground 0

Field peas:
  with snaps, frozen *(Southland)* 0

Fig:
   fresh, canned, or dried   0

Filbert:
   raw, dried, or roasted   0

Finnan haddie, see "Haddock, smoked"

Fish, see specific listings

Fish fillet dinner, frozen:
   divan *(Lean Cuisine)*, 12³/₈ oz.   85
   Florentine *(Lean Cuisine)*, 9 oz. 100
   jardiniere *(Lean Cuisine)*, 11¼ oz. 100

Fish sticks, frozen:
   reheated, 4 oz. 127
   reheated, 1 stick, 4″ × 1″ × ¹/₂″   31

Flatfish, see "Flounder" and "Sole"

Flounder:
   raw, meat only, 4 oz.   54
   raw, 1 fillet, 5.7 oz. (from 2-lb. whole fish)   78
   baked or broiled, meat only, 4 oz.   77
   baked or broiled, 1 fillet, 4.5 oz. (5.7 oz. raw)   86

Flour:
   all grain, nut, seed, and vegetable varieties . . .   0

Frankfurters and weiners:
   (Armour Star Jumbo), 2-oz. link   30
   (Oscar Mayer Little Weiners), ¹/₃-oz. link   5
   (Oscar Mayer Weiners), 1.6-oz. link   27

Frankfurters and weiners *(cont.)*

all meat *(Armour Star* Giant), 1.6-oz. link	25
all meat *(Armour Star* Giant), 2-oz. link	28
all meat *(Armour Star* Great 8), 2-oz. link	28
bacon and Cheddar *(Oscar Mayer* Hot Dogs), 1.6-oz. link	30
beef, 1.6-oz. link (10 per 1-lb. pkg.)	22
beef, 2-oz. link (8 per 1-lb. pkg.)	27
beef *(Armour Star),* 1.6-oz. link	20
beef *(Armour Star),* 2-oz. link	25
beef *(Armour Star* Giant), 2-oz. link	25
beef *(Armour Star* Jumbo), 2-oz. link	30
beef *(Hillshire Farm* Old Fashioned), 1-oz. link	7
beef *(Oscar Mayer),* 1.6-oz. link	27
beef and pork, 1.6-oz. link (10 per 1-lb. pkg.)	22
beef and pork, 2-oz. link (8 per 1-lb. pkg.) . . .	29
cheese *(Oscar Mayer* Hot Dogs), 1.6-oz. link	30
cheese, nacho style *(Oscar Mayer* Hot Dogs), 1.6-oz. link	30
cheese smokie, pork and beef, 2-oz. link	19
cheese smokie, pork and beef, 1.5-oz. link . . .	29
chicken, see "Chicken frankfurter"	
turkey, see "Turkey frankfurter"	

Fructose:

(Estee)	0

Fruit, see specific listings

Fruit, candied:

all varieties	0

Fruit, mixed:

canned, dried, or frozen	0

Fruit bars, frozen:
    all flavors *(Good Humor Lite Stix)*   0
    all fruit flavors *(Dole Fruit 'n Juice)*   0
    lemonade or orange *(Sunkist)*   0

Fruit beverages, see specific listings

Fruit blend juice or drink:
    all varieties, canned, mix, or frozen   0

Fruit and nut mix:
    (Planters)   0

Fruit punch, see "Fruit blend juice or drink"

Fuki, see "Butterbur"

G

Food and Measure	Cholesterol (mgs.)

Garbanzos, see "Chick peas"

Garden salad:
marinated, canned *(S&W)* 0

Garlic:
fresh 0

Garlic dip:
(Kraft) 0
(Nalley's), 1 oz. 17

Garlic powder:
plain or parslied 0

Garlic salt:
   regular or salt substitute   0

Gefilte fish:
   canned or in jars with broth, drained, 4 oz. . . .   34
   canned or in jars with broth, 1½-oz. piece . . .   12

Gelatin:
   unflavored *(Knox)*   0

Gelatin dessert mix:
   all flavors, prepared with water   0

Gelatin drink:
   orange flavor *(Knox)*   0

Giblets (see also "Gizzard," "Heart," and "Liver"):
   capon:
     raw, giblets from 6.5-lb. raw capon, 4.1 oz.   335
     simmered, drained, chopped, or diced, ½
       cup   315
   chicken, broilers, or fryers:
     raw, giblets from 3.3-lb. raw chicken, 2.6 oz.   196
     fried*, chopped or diced, ½ cup   324
     simmered, drained, chopped or diced, ½
       cup   285
   chicken, roasters:
     raw, giblets from 4.5-lb. raw chicken, 4 oz.   267
     simmered, drained, chopped or diced, ½
       cup   259

*** Flour-coated; fried in vegetable shortening**

Giblets *(cont.)*
  chicken, stewing:
    raw, giblets from 2.9-lb. raw chicken, 2.9 oz.   195
    simmered, drained, chopped or diced, 1/2
      cup.   258
  turkey:
    raw, giblets from 15.5-lb. raw turkey, 8.6 oz.   688
    simmered, drained, chopped or diced, 1/2
      cup.   303

Gin, see "Liquor"

Ginger:
  root, fresh, dried or ground   0

Gizzard:
  chicken, fresh:
    braised or simmered, 1 oz.   55
    braised or simmered, chopped or diced, 1/2
      cup.   141
  turkey, fresh:
    braised or simmered, 1 oz.   66
    braised or simmered, chopped or diced, 1/2
      cup.   168

Godfather's Pizza:
  original pizza, 1 slice:
    cheese, 1/4 of mini pie   8
    cheese, 1/6 of small pie   15
    cheese, 1/8 of medium pie   15
    cheese, 1/10 of large pie   20
    cheese, hot slice, 1/8 of large pie   25
    combo, 1/4 of mini pie   10
    combo, 1/6 of small pie   30

Godfather's Pizza, original pizza, 1 slice *(cont.)*
    combo, 1/8 of medium pie 35
    combo, 1/10 of large pie 36
    combo, hot slice, 1/8 of large pie 45
  stuffed pie pizza, 1 slice:
    cheese, 1/6 of small pie 25
    cheese, 1/8 of medium pie 25
    cheese, 1/10 of large pie 32
    combo, 1/6 of small pie 40
    combo, 1/6 of medium pie 43
    combo, 1/10 of large pie 48
  thin crust pizza, 1 slice:
    cheese, 1/6 of small pie 10
    cheese, 1/8 of medium pie 14
    cheese, 1/10 of large pie 16
    combo, 1/6 of small pie 25
    combo, 1/8 of medium pie 25
    combo, 1/10 of large pie 27

Goose, edible portions:
  domestic, raw:
    meat and skin, 11.3 oz. (yield per 1 lb. with
      bone) 256
    meat and skin, 1/2 goose (3.5 lb. with bone)   1,055
  domestic, roasted:
    meat and skin, 6.6 oz. (yield per 1 lb. raw
      with bone) 172
    meat and skin, 1/2 goose (2.4 lb. with bone)   708
    meat only, 4 oz. 109

Goose fat:
  raw, 1 cup 205
  raw, 1 tbsp. 13

Goose liver pâté, see "Pâté"

Gooseberries:
fresh or canned   0

Gourd:
all varieties, fresh or dried   0

Granola, see "Cereal, ready-to-eat"

Grape:
all varieties, fresh or canned   0

Grape juice or drink:
canned, chilled, frozen, or mix   0

Grape roll or bar:
natural or sweetened   0

Grapefruit:
all varieties, fresh or canned   0

Grapefruit juice:
fresh, canned, or frozen   0

Grapeseed oil, see "Oil"

Grenadine:
(Rose's)   0

Ground cherry:
fresh   0

Grouper:
mixed species:
    raw, meat only, 4 oz. 42
    raw, 1 fillet, 9.1 oz. (from 3-lb. whole fish) . . 95
    baked or broiled, meat only, 4 oz. 53
    baked or broiled, 1 fillet, 7.1 oz. (9.1 oz. raw) 95

Guacamole dip:
(Kraft Guacamole) 0
(Nalley's Avocado Dip/Guacamole), 1 oz. 14

Guava:
common or strawberry, fresh 0

Guava juice:
canned or bottled 0

Guava sauce:
cooked 0

Guinea hen:
raw, meat only, 9.7 oz. (yield per 1 lb. with
    bone) 173
raw, meat only, 4 oz. 71

H

Food and Measure	Cholesterol (mgs.)

Haddock:
  fresh:
    raw, meat only, 4 oz.   65
    raw, 1 fillet, 6.8 oz. (from 2½-lb. whole fish) 111
    baked or broiled, meat only, 4 oz.   84
    baked or broiled, 1 fillet, 5.3 oz. (6.8 oz. raw) 110
  smoked, meat only, 4 oz.   87

Hake, see "Whiting"

Halibut:
  Atlantic and Pacific:
    raw, meat only, 4 oz.   36
    raw, ½ fillet, 7.2 oz. (from 5-lb. whole fish)   65
    baked or broiled, meat only, 4 oz.   46

Halibut, Atlantic and Pacific *(cont.)*
  baked or broiled, 1/2 fillet, 5.6 oz. (7.2 oz.
  raw)   65
  Greenland:
  raw, meat only, 4 oz.   52
  raw, 1/2 fillet, 7.2 oz. (from 5-lb. whole fish)   94

Ham, edible portions:
  fresh, whole, roasted (with bone and skin):
  lean with fat, 4 oz.   105
  lean with fat, chopped or diced, 1 cup or 4.9
  oz.   131
  lean only (fat trimmed), 4 oz.   77
  lean only, chopped or diced, 1 cup or 4.9 oz.   131
  fresh, rump half, roasted (with bone and skin):
  lean with fat, 4 oz.   108
  lean with fat, chopped or diced, 1 cup or 4.9
  oz.   133
  lean only (fat trimmed), 4 oz.   109
  lean only, chopped or diced, 1 cup or 4.9 oz.   134
  fresh, shank half, roasted (with bone and skin):
  lean with fat, 4 oz.   104
  lean with fat, chopped or diced, 1 cup or 4.9
  oz.   129
  lean only (fat trimmed), 4 oz.   104
  lean only, chopped or diced, 1 cup or 4.9 oz.   129
  cured, whole, unheated (fully cooked):
  lean with fat, 4 oz.   64
  lean with fat, chopped or diced, 1 cup or 4.9
  oz.   78
  lean only (fat trimmed), 4 oz.   59
  lean only, chopped or diced, 1 cup or 4.9 oz.   73
  cured, whole, roasted:
  lean with fat, 4 oz.   70

Ham, cured, whole, roasted *(cont.)*

lean with fat, chopped or diced, 1 cup or 4.9
oz. 86

lean only (fat trimmed), 4 oz. 62

lean only, chopped or diced, 1 cup or 4.9 oz. 78

cured, shoulder, blade roll:

unheated, lean with fat, 4 oz. 60

roasted, lean with fat, 4 oz. 76

cured, shoulder, arm picnic:

unheated, lean with fat, 4 oz. 66

unheated, lean with fat, chopped or diced,
1 cup or 4.9 oz. 82

roasted, lean only (fat trimmed), 4 oz. 54

roasted, lean only, chopped or diced, 1 cup
or 4.9 oz. 68

cured, boneless, unheated (fully cooked):

extra lean, 4 oz. 53

extra lean, chopped or diced, 1 cup or 4.9
oz. 66

regular, 4 oz. 65

regular, chopped or diced, 1 cup or 4.9 oz. 80

cured, boneless, roasted:

extra lean, 4 oz. 60

extra lean, chopped or diced, 1 cup or 4.9
oz. 74

regular, 4 oz. 67

regular, chopped or diced, 1 cup or 4.9 oz. 83

Ham, canned:

extra lean, unheated, 3 oz. 32

extra lean, roasted, 3 oz. 25

regular, unheated, 3 oz. 33

regular, roasted, 3 oz. 52

(Armour Golden Star), 3 oz. 50

Ham, canned *(cont.)*
(Armour Star/Armour Star Nugget), 3 oz.	50
(Oscar Mayer Jubilee), 3 oz.	38
chopped, 3 oz.	42
chopped, 3/4-oz. slice	10
chopped *(Armour Star)*, 3 oz.	50

Ham, sliced and luncheon meat:
1-oz. slice	16
(Armour Lower Salt), 1 oz.	16
(Armour Star Speedy Cut), 1 oz.	14
(Oscar Mayer Jubilee), 1 oz.	15
(Oscar Mayer Jubilee Slices), 1 oz.	13
chopped:	
3/4-oz. slice	11
1-oz. slice	15
(Armour), 1-oz. slice	15
(Oscar Mayer), 1-oz. slice	14
cracked black pepper *(Oscar Mayer)*, 1-oz. slice	11
extra lean, 1-oz. slice	13
honey *(Oscar Mayer)*, 1-oz. slice	11
Italian style *(Oscar Mayer)*, 1-oz. slice	9
minced, 3/4-oz. slice	15
minced, 1-oz. slice	20
smoked:	
(Carl Buddig), 1 oz.	20
cooked *(Oscar Mayer)*, 1-oz. slice	10
turkey, see "Turkey ham"	

Ham and cheese loaf:
1-oz. slice	16
(Oscar Mayer), 1-oz. slice	17

Ham and cheese spread:

1 oz.	17
1 tbsp.	9
(Oscar Mayer), 1 oz.	16

Ham patties, canned or uncanned:

unheated or grilled, 1 oz.	20
unheated, 1 patty, 2.3 oz.	46
grilled, 1 patty, 2.1 oz. (2.3 oz. unheated)	43

Ham salad spread:

1 oz.	10
1 tbsp.	6
(Oscar Mayer), 1 oz.	11

Ham steak:

cured, extra lean, unheated, 2-oz. slice	26
(Oscar Mayer Jubilee), 2 oz.	27

Hamburger, see "Beef" and specific fast-food restaurants

Hardee's:

breakfast, 1 serving:

bacon and egg biscuit, 4 oz.	305
biscuit, cinnamon 'n raisin, 2.7 oz.	< 1
biscuit gravy, 4 oz.	21
country ham biscuit, 3.4 oz.	12
egg, 1.2 oz.	160
Hash Rounds, 2.5 oz.	10
sausage biscuit, 4 oz.	17
steak biscuit, 5 oz.	16

sandwiches, 1 serving:

bacon cheeseburger, 7.3 oz.	60

Hardee's, sandwiches *(cont.)*
  Big Deluxe, 7.4 oz.   50
  cheeseburger, 4.1 oz.   28
  cheeseburger, 1/4 lb., 6.5 oz.   77
  chicken fillet, 6.8 oz.   57
  Fisherman's Fillet, 7 oz.   80
  Hot Ham 'N' Cheese, 5.3 oz.   59
  Hot Ham 'N' Cheese, with lettuce and
    tomato, 6.6 oz.   43
  Mushroom 'N' Swiss, 7.3 oz.   86
  roast beef, 4.6 oz.   46
  Turkey Club, 6.9 oz.   45
  salads and side dishes, 1 serving:
    chef salad, 12 oz.   179
    French fries, large, 4.3 oz. . . . .   tr.
    shrimp 'n pasta salad, 11.75 oz.   293
    side salad, 4.2 oz. . . . .   < 1
  desserts and shakes, 1 serving:
    apple turnover, 3.1 oz. . . . .   tr.
    big cookie, 1.9 oz.   9
    milkshake, 11.6 oz. . . . .   < 1

Hazelnut, see "Filbert"

Hazelnut oil, see "Oil"

Head cheese:
  1-oz. slice   23
  (Oscar Mayer), 1 oz.   21

Heart:
  fresh, braised or simmered:
    beef, 4 oz.   219
    chicken, 4 oz.   274

Heart, fresh, braised or simmered *(cont.)*

chicken, 1 heart (.2 oz. raw)	7
chicken, 1 cup or 5.1 oz.	350
pork, 4 oz.	251
pork, 1 cup	320
turkey, 4 oz.	256
turkey, 1 cup	327

Herbs, see specific listings

Herbs, mixed:

(Lawry's Pinch of Herbs)	0

Herring:

Atlantic, fresh:

raw, meat only, 4 oz.	68
raw, 1 fillet, 6.8 oz. (from 1 1/2-lb. whole fish)	110
baked or broiled, meat only, 4 oz.	87
baked or broiled, 1 fillet, 5 oz. (6.8 oz. raw)	110

Atlantic, kippered:

4 oz.	93
1 fillet (4 3/8" × 1 3/4" × 1/4"), 1.4 oz.	33

Atlantic, pickled:

4 oz.	15
1 piece (1 3/4" × 7/8" × 1/2"), .5 oz.	2

lake, smoked, see "Cisco"

Pacific, fresh:

raw, meat only, 4 oz.	87
raw, 1 fillet, 6.5 oz. (from 1 1/2-lb. whole fish)	141
round, meat only, 4 oz.	32

Herring oil:

1 oz.	217

Hickory nuts:
raw or dried   0

Hollandaise sauce mix:
dehydrated, with butterfat:
    dry form, 1.2-oz. pkg.   40
    prepared with water, 1 cup   51
dehydrated, with vegetable oil:
    dry form, .9-oz. pkg. . . . .   tr.
    prepared with milk and butter, 1 cup   189

Hominy, see "Corn grits"

Honey:
all varieties, strained or extracted   0

Honey loaf:
(Oscar Mayer), 1-oz. slice   12
pork and beef, 1-oz. slice   10

Honey roll sausage:
beef, 1 oz.   14
beef, 1 slice, 4″ diam. × 1/8″ thick   12

Honeydew:
fresh   0

Horseradish:
fresh or prepared, without cream   0

Horseradish sauce:
(Sauceworks), 1 tbsp.   5

Hot dogs, see "Frankfurters and weiners"

Hot sauce, see "Pepper sauce" and specific
  listings

Hull peas:
purple, raw or frozen 0

Hummus:
commercial or home recipe 0
mix, dry *(Casbah)* 0

Hyacinth beans:
raw 0

I

Food and Measure	Cholesterol (mgs.)

Ice, flavored:

all flavors, without cream	0

Ice bars:

all flavors (*Eskimo* Twin Pops)	0
all flavors (*Fla-Vor-Ice*)	0
all flavors (*Pop-Ice*)	0

Ice cream:

butter almond (*Flav-O-Rich*), 1/2 cup	27
butter pecan (*Flav-O-Rich*), 1/2 cup	27
cherry vanilla (*Flav-O-Rich*), 1/2 cup	25
chocolate (*Flav-O-Rich*), 1/2 cup	29
chocolate chip (*Flav-O-Rich*), 1/2 cup	27
coconut (*Flav-O-Rich*), 1/2 cup	26
coffee (*Flav-O-Rich*), 1/2 cup	28

Ice cream *(cont.)*

coffee, Colombian *(Flav-O-Rich Rich &
Creamy)*, 1/2 cup   34
cookies 'n cream *(Flav-O-Rich)*, 1/2 cup   25
fudge, ripple *(Flav-O-Rich)*, 1/2 cup   25
heavenly hash *(Flav-O-Rich)*, 1/2 cup   26
moon pie *(Flav-O-Rich)*, 1/2 cup   25
Neapolitan *(Flav-O-Rich)*, 1/2 cup   27
peach *(Flav-O-Rich)*, 1/2 cup   24
peach *(Flav-O-Rich Rich & Creamy)*, 1/2 cup . .   27
rocky road *(Flav-O-Rich)*, 1/2 cup   27
spumoni *(Flav-O-Rich)*, 1/2 cup   26
strawberries 'n cream *(Flav-O-Rich)*, 1/2 cup . .   20
strawberry *(Flav-O-Rich)*, 1/2 cup   25
strawberry cheesecake *(Flav-O-Rich Rich &
Creamy)*, 1/2 cup   31
vanilla:
regular (about 11% fat), hardened, 1/2 cup   30
regular (about 11% fat), soft-serve, 1/2 cup   7
rich (about 16% fat), hardened, 1/2 cup   44
(Flav-O-Rich), 1/2 cup   28
(Land O Lakes), 1/2 cup   30
old-fashioned *(Flav-O-Rich Rich & Creamy)*,
1/2 cup   34
vanilla-Swiss chocolate almond
(Flav-O-Rich Rich & Creamy), 1/2 cup   27
walnut, black *(Flav-O-Rich)*, 1/2 cup   27

Ice cream, non-dairy:
all flavors *(Mocha Mix)*   0

Ice cream cones and cups, plain:
cones, sugar *(Comet)*   0
cups, all flavors *(Comet)*   0

Ice milk:
  vanilla, hardened, 1/2 cup   9
  vanilla, soft-serve, 1/2 cup   7
  vanilla *(Land O Lakes)*, 1/2 cup   10

Ice sherbet, see "Sherbet"

Italian sausage, see "Sausage"

J

Jack mackerel, see "Mackerel"

Jack-in-the-Box:
  breakfast, 1 serving:
    bacon, 2 slices 10
    breakfast Jack 203
    Canadian crescent 226
    eggs, scrambled, breakfast 260
    pancake breakfast 85
    sausage crescent 187
    supreme crescent 178
  sandwiches, salads, and dinners, 1 serving:
    bacon cheeseburger supreme 70
    cheeseburger 42
    chicken strips dinner 100
    chicken supreme 60

Jack-in-the-Box, sandwiches, salads, dinners *(cont.)*

club pita	43
ham and Swiss burger	117
hamburger	29
jumbo Jack	64
jumbo Jack with cheese	110
Moby Jack	47
mushroom burger	87
pasta seafood salad	48
shrimp salad	139
sirloin steak dinner	75
Swiss and bacon burger	99
taco, regular	21
taco, super	37
taco salad	102

nachos and side dishes, 1 serving:

French fries, regular	8
nachos, cheese	37
nachos, supreme	55
onion rings	27

desserts and shakes, 1 serving:

apple turnover	15
shake, chocolate, strawberry, or vanilla	25

Jackfruit:

fresh	0

Jalapeño, see "Pepper, jalapeño"

Jalapeño dip:

(Fritos), 3 1/8 oz.	5
(Kraft)	0
(Kraft Premium), 1 oz.	15
(Nalley's), 1 oz.	16

Jams and preserves:
  all varieties 0

Java plum:
  fresh 0

Jelly:
  all varieties 0

Jerusalem artichoke:
  fresh 0

Jujube:
  fresh or dried 0

Juki, see "Butterbur"

K

Food and Measure	Cholesterol (mgs.)

Kale:
fresh or frozen 0

Kale, Scotch:
fresh 0

Kasha:
medium or whole *(Wolff's)* 0

Kentucky Fried Chicken:
chicken, original recipe:
   breast, center, 3.8 oz. 93
   breast, side, 3.4 oz. 96
   drumstick, 2.1 oz. 81
   thigh, 3.4 oz. 122
   wing, 2 oz. 67

Kentucky Fried Chicken *(cont.)*

chicken, extra crispy:

breast, center, 4.2 oz.	93
breast, side, 3.5 oz.	66
drumstick, 2.1 oz.	65
thigh, 3.9 oz.	121
wing, 2 oz.	63
chicken, Kentucky nuggets, .6-oz. piece	12

Kentucky nugget sauces:

barbecue, 1 oz.	< 1
honey, .5 oz.	< 1
mustard, 1 oz.	< 1
sweet and sour, 1 oz.	< 1
chicken gravy, 2.8 oz.	2

side dishes, 1 serving:

baked beans, 3.1 oz.	< 1
buttermilk biscuit, 2.6-oz. piece	< 1
cole slaw, 2.8 oz.	4
corn-on-the-cob, 5 oz.	< 1
Kentucky fries, 4.2 oz.	< 2
mashed potatoes, 2.8 oz.	< 1
mashed potatoes with gravy, 3 oz.	< 1
potato salad, 3.2 oz.	11

Kidney:

beef, raw, 4 oz.	322
beef, braised, 4 oz.	439
pork, raw, 4 oz.	362
pork, braised, 4 oz.	544

Kielbasa, see "Polish sausage"

Kiwi fruit:

fresh	0

Knockwurst:
  (Hillshire Farm), 1 oz.   12
  pork and beef, 2.4-oz. link, 4″ long × 1 1/8″
    diam.   39
  pork and beef, 1 oz.   16

Kohlrabi:
  fresh   0

Kumquat:
  fresh   0

L

Lake herring, see "Cisco"

Lamb, retail trim, edible portion:
chop, 1 (3 per lb. with bone):

arm, braised, lean with fat, 2.2 oz.	77
arm, braised, lean only (fat trimmed), 1.7 oz.	59
loin, broiled, lean with fat, 2.8 oz.	78
loin, broiled, lean only (fat trimmed), 2.3 oz.	60

leg, roasted, 2 slices, 4¹/₈″ × 2¹/₄″ × ¹/₄″:

lean with fat, 3 oz.	78
lean only (fat trimmed), 2.6 oz.	65

rib, roasted, 3 pieces, 2¹/₂″ × 2¹/₂″ × ¹/₄″:

lean with fat, 3 oz.	77
lean only (fat trimmed), 2 oz.	50

Lambs-quarters:
  fresh   0

Lard, see "Pork lard"

Lasagna, canned:
  (Nalley's), 3 1/2 oz.   5

Lasagna dinner, frozen:
  (Dinner Classics), 10 oz.   75
  tofu, see "Tofu entrées"
  tuna *(Lean Cuisine)*, 9 3/4 oz.   25
  zucchini *(Lean Cuisine)*, 11 oz.   20

Lebanon bologna, see "Bologna"

Lecithin, see "Soybean lecithin"

Leeks:
  fresh or freeze-dried   0

Lemon:
  fresh   0

Lemon extract:
  (Virginia Dare)   0

Lemon juice:
  fresh, frozen, or reconstituted   0

Lemon pepper:
  (Lawry's)   0

Lemon-lime drink:
  fresh, frozen, or mix   0

Lemonade:
  fresh, canned, frozen, or mix   0

Lentil:
  dried, whole or split   0

Lentil pilaf mix:
  with rice, dry *(Casbah)*   0

Lettuce:
  all varieties, fresh   0

Lichee nuts:
  raw or dried   0

Lime:
  fresh   0

Lime juice:
  fresh, frozen, or reconstituted   0

Limeade:
  fresh or frozen   0

Linseed oil, see "Oil"

Lingcod:
  raw, meat only, 4 oz.   59
  raw, 1/2 fillet, 6.8 oz. (from 5-lb. whole fish) . . .   100

Linguine dinner, frozen:
 with clam sauce *(Lean Cuisine)*, 9⅝ oz.   40

Liquor:
 distilled, all varieties (bourbon, brandy, gin,
  Scotch, rye, rum, vodka, etc.), all proofs . . .   0

Liver:
 beef, raw, 4 oz.   402
 beef, pan-fried, 4 oz.   547
 chicken, raw, 4 oz.   498
 chicken, braised or simmered, 4 oz.   716
 chicken, braised or simmered, chopped or
  diced, 1 cup   883
 duck, domesticated, raw, 4 oz.   584
 duck, domesticated, raw, 1 liver, 1.6 oz.   227
 pork, raw, 4 oz.   341
 pork, braised or simmered, 4 oz.   403
 turkey, raw, 4 oz.   528
 turkey, braised or simmered, 4 oz.   710
 turkey, braised or simmered, chopped or diced,
  1 cup   876

Liver cheese:
 (Oscar Mayer), 1⅜-oz. slice   75
 pork, 1.3-oz. slice (6 per 18-oz. pkg.)   66
 pork, 1 oz.   49

Liver pâté, see "Pâté"

Liver sausage, see "Braunschweiger"

Liverwurst:
 (Armour Star), 1 oz.   45

Liverwurst *(cont.)*
   pork, 1 oz. 45
   pork, .6-oz. slice, 2½" diam. × ¼" 28

Lobster:
   northern:
     raw, meat only, 4 oz. 108
     raw, meat only, 5.3 oz. (from 1½-lb. whole
      lobster) 143
     steamed or boiled, meat only, 4 oz. 82
     steamed or boiled, meat only, 1 cup or 5.1
      oz. 104
   European, raw, meat only, 4 oz. 146
   spiny, see "Spiny lobster"

Loganberries:
   fresh or canned 0

Longan:
   fresh or dried 0

Loquat:
   fresh 0

Lotus seeds:
   fresh or dried 0

Lox, see "Salmon, Chinook, smoked"

Luncheon meat (see also specific listings):
   (Oscar Mayer), 1-oz. slice 16
   pork and beef, 1-oz. slice 15
   sausage, pork and beef, 1-oz. slice 18

Luncheon meat *(cont.)*
    sausage, pork and beef, 1 slice (10 per 8-oz.
       pkg.)   15
    spiced *(Armour)*, 1-oz. slice   20
    spiced, with chicken *(Armour Star)*, 3 oz.   70

Luxury loaf:
    (Oscar Mayer), 1-oz. slice   13

M

Food and Measure	Cholesterol (mgs.)
Macadamia nuts:	
fresh, dried, or roasted	0
Macaroni:	
all varieties, dry	0
Macaroni and beef, canned:	
(*Nalley's*), 3 1/2 oz.	10
Macaroni and cheese, mix*:	
(*Kraft* Dinner), 3/4 cup	5
(*Kraft* Deluxe Dinner), 3/4 cup	20
(*Kraft* Family Size Dinner), 3/4 cup	5
shells (*Velveeta* Dinner), 3/4 cup	25
spiral (*Kraft* Dinner), 3/4 cup	10

* Prepared according to package directions

Mace:
  whole or ground   0

Mackerel:
Atlantic:
  raw, meat only, 4 oz.   79
  raw, 1 fillet, 3.9 oz. (from 1½-lb. whole fish)   78
  baked or broiled, meat only, 4 oz.   85
  baked or broiled, 1 fillet, 3.1 oz. (3.9 oz. raw)   66
chub, raw, meat only, 4 oz.   59
horse, raw, meat only, 4 oz.   46
horse, Japanese, raw, meat only, 4 oz.   54
jack and Pacific, fresh:
  raw, meat only, 4 oz.   53
  raw, 1 fillet, 7.9 oz. (from 3-lb. whole fish) . .   106
jack, canned, drained:
  1 cup or 6.7 oz.   150
  4 oz.   90
king:
  raw, meat only, 4 oz.   60
  raw, ½ fillet, 7 oz. (from 5-lb. whole fish) . .   106
Spanish:
  raw, meat only, 4 oz.   86
  raw, 1 fillet, 6.6 oz. (from 2½-lb. whole fish)   142
  baked or broiled, meat only, 4 oz.   83
  baked or broiled, 1 fillet, 5.1 oz. (6.6 oz. raw)   107

Mai tai cocktail:
  fluid or mix   0

Malt:
  dry   0

Malt extract:
  dry   0

Malt liquor, see "Beer, ale, and malt liquor"

Malted milk, see "Milk, malted"

Mango:
  fresh   0

Manhattan cocktail:
  fluid or mix   0

Maple syrup:
  pure or blended   0

Margarine:
  made with vegetable or seed oil, regular or soft   0

Margarine-butter blend:
  regular or soft *(Blue Bonnet* Butter Blend),
    1 tbsp.   5
  regular or soft *(Country Morning Blend),* 1 tbsp.   10

Margarita cocktail:
  fluid, frozen, or mix   0

Marjoram:
  fresh or dried   0

Marmalade:
  all varieties   0

Marmalade plum, see "Sapote"

Martini cocktail:
  fluid or mix. 0

Matzo, see "Cracker"

Matzo meal, see "Cracker crumbs and meal"

Mayonnaise:
  (Best Foods/Hellmann's), 1 tbsp. 5
  (Cains), 1 tbsp. 10
  (Kraft/Kraft Light), 1 tbsp. 5
  (Mother's), 1 tbsp. 10
  (Mrs. Filbert's), 1 tbsp. 10
  (Nalley's), 1 tbsp. 11
  (Rokeach), 1 tbsp. 10
  (Weight Watchers Reduced Calorie/Low
    Sodium), 1 tbsp. 5
  soybean, 1/2 cup 65
  soybean, 1 tbsp. 8

Mayonnaise, imitation:
  (Featherweight Soyamaise) 0
  (Mrs. Filbert's) 0
  milk cream, 1/2 cup 52
  milk cream, 1 tbsp. 6
  soybean, 1/2 cup 29
  soybean, 1 tbsp. 4
  soybean, cholesterol-free 0

Mayonnaise-type dressing, see "Salad
dressing, bottled"

McDonald's:

breakfast, 1 serving:

biscuit, plain, 3 oz. 9

biscuit with bacon, egg, and cheese, 5.2 oz.   262

biscuit with sausage, 4.3 oz. 48

biscuit with sausage and egg, 6.25 oz. 285

Egg McMuffin, 4.9 oz. 259

eggs, scrambled, 3.5 oz. 514

English muffin with butter, 2.25 oz. 15

hash brown potatoes, 2 oz. 7

hotcakes with butter and syrup, 7.6 oz. 47

sausage, 2 oz. 39

Sausage McMuffin, 4.1 oz. 59

Sausage McMuffin with egg, 5.8 oz. 287

sandwiches and chicken, 1 serving:

Big Mac, 7.1 oz. 83

cheeseburger, 4 oz. 41

Chicken McNuggets, 3.8 oz. 73

Chicken McNuggets sauces:

    barbecue sauce, 1.1 oz. . . . . < 1

    honey sauce, .5 oz. . . . . < 1

    hot mustard sauce, 1.1 oz. 3

    sweet & sour sauce, 1.1 oz. . . . . < 1

Filet-O-Fish, 5.1 oz. 45

hamburger, 3.5 oz. 29

Quarter Pounder, 5.7 oz. 81

Quarter Pounder with cheese, 6.6 oz. 107

French fries, regular, 2.4 oz. 9

desserts and shakes, 1 serving:

apple pie, 3 oz. 12

cherry pie, 3.1 oz. 13

cones, 4 oz. 23

cookies, chocolate chip, 2.4 oz. 18

cookies, *McDonaldland,* 2.4 oz. 10

McDonald's, desserts and shakes, 1 serving *(cont.)*
    milk shake, chocolate, 10.3 oz. 30
    milk shake, strawberry, 10.3 oz. 32
    milk shake, vanilla, 10.3 oz. 31
    sundae, caramel, 5.8 oz. 31
    sundae, hot fudge, 5.8 oz. 27
    sundae, strawberry, 5.8 oz. 25

Meat, see specific listings

Meat, luncheon, see "Luncheon meat" and
  specific listings

Meat-fish-poultry sauce, see "Steak sauce"

Meat loaf, turkey, see "Turkey meat loaf"

Meat loaf sauce:
    canned *(Hunt's Meatloaf Fixins)* 0

Meat seasoning:
    (Lawry's Natural Choice for Meat) 0

Meatball dinner, frozen:
    stew *(Lean Cuisine),* 10 oz. 65
    Swedish *(Dinner Classics),* 11½ oz. 125

Meatball stew:
    canned *(Nalley's),* 3½ oz. 20

Melon, see specific listings

Melon balls, mixed:
    fresh or frozen 0

Mettwurst:
   (Hillshire Farm), 1-oz. slice   7

Milk, fluid:
  buttermilk:
    sweet cream, 8 fl. oz.   83
    sweet cream, 1 tbsp.   5
    (Flav-O-Rich), 8 fl. oz.   6
    (Flav-O-Rich, 3.25% fat), 8 fl. oz.   35
    (Flav-O-Rich, 3.5% fat), 8 fl. oz.   38
    (Land O Lakes), 8 fl. oz.   10
  condensed, sweetened, 8 fl. oz.   104
  condensed, sweetened, 1 fl. oz.   13
  evaporated, canned:
    skim, 8 fl. oz.   10
    skim, 1 fl. oz.   1
    whole, 8 fl. oz.   74
    whole, 1 fl. oz.   9
  filled, 8 fl. oz.   4
  lowfat:
    .5% fat *(Flav-O-Rich)*, 8 fl. oz.   9
    1% fat, 8 fl. oz.   10
    1% fat, with nonfat milk solids, 8 fl. oz.   10
    1% fat, protein fortified, 8 fl. oz.   10
    1% fat *(Flav-O-Rich)*, 8 fl. oz.   13
    1% fat *(Land O Lakes)*, 8 fl. oz.   10
    2% fat, 8 fl. oz.   18
    2% fat, with nonfat milk solids, 8 fl. oz.   18
    2% fat, protein fortified, 8 fl. oz.   19
    2% fat *(Flav-O-Rich)*, 8 fl. oz.   23
    2% fat *(Land O Lakes)*, 8 fl. oz.   20
    (Flav-O-Rich Sweet Acidophilus), 8 fl. oz. . .   13

Milk *(cont.)*
skim:
  8 fl. oz. 4
  with nonfat milk solids, 8 fl. oz. 5
  protein fortified, 8 fl. oz. 5
  (Flav-O-Rich/Flav-O-Rich Weight Watchers),
    8 fl. oz. 4
  (Land O Lakes), 8 fl. oz. 5
whole:
  3.3% fat, 8 fl. oz. 33
  3.5% fat *(Flav-O-Rich)*, 8 fl. oz. 37
  low sodium, 8 fl. oz. 33
  producer, 3.7% fat, 8 fl. oz. 35
  (Flav-O-Rich), 8 fl. oz. 35
  (Land O Lakes), 8 fl. oz. 35

Milk, dry:
buttermilk, sweet cream, 1 cup 83
buttermilk, sweet cream, 1 tbsp. 5
nonfat, regular, 1 cup 24
nonfat, instant, 1 envelope, 3.2 oz. 17
whole, regular, 1 cup 124

Milk, chocolate, dairy:
lowfat milk:
  (Land O Lakes), 8 fl. oz. 5
  1% fat, 8 fl. oz. 7
  1% fat *(Flav-O-Rich/Farm Best)*, 8 fl. oz. ... 13
  2% fat, 8 fl. oz. 17
  2% fat *(Flav-O-Rich/Farm Best)*, 8 fl. oz. ... 23
skim milk *(Land O Lakes)*, 8 fl. oz. 5
whole milk:
  8 fl. oz. 30
  (Flav-O-Rich/Farm Best), 8 fl. oz. 36

Milk, chocolate, dairy, whole milk *(cont.)*
   (Land O Lakes), 8 fl. oz.   30
   3.5% fat *(Flav-O-Rich/Farm Best)*, 8 fl. oz.   38

Milk, chocolate, mix:
   powder   0
   prepared with whole milk, 8 fl. oz.   33

Milk, goat's:
   whole, 8 fl. oz.   28

Milk, imitation:
   8 fl. oz. . . . .   tr.

Milk, Indian buffalo:
   whole, 8 fl. oz.   46

Milk, malted:
   chocolate flavor:
      dry powder   0
      prepared with whole milk, 8 fl. oz.   34
   natural flavor:
      dry powder, 3 heaping tsp. or 3/4 oz.   4
      prepared with whole milk, 8 fl. oz.   37
   strawberry flavor mix:
      dry powder   0
      prepared with whole milk, 8 fl. oz.   33

Milk fish:
   raw, meat only, 4 oz.   59

Millet:
   whole grain   0

Mincemeat, see "Pie filling"

Miso, see "Soybean, fermented"

Molasses:
　all varieties   0

Monkfish:
　raw, meat only, 4 oz.   28

Mortadella:
　beef and pork, 1 oz.   16
　beef and pork, 1 slice (15 per 8-oz. pkg.)   8

Mother's loaf:
　pork, 1 oz.   13
　pork, 1 slice, 4¹/₄″ × 4¹/₄″ × ¹/₁₆″   9

Muffins:
　all varieties *(Thomas' Toast-r-Cakes)*   0
　English:
　　(Roman Meal)   0
　　(Thomas')   0
　　(Wonder)   0
　　honey wheat, raisin, or sourdough *(Thomas')*   0
　raisin *(Wonder Raisin Rounds)*   0
　sourdough *(Wonder)*   0

Muffins, frozen:
　all varieties *(Sara Lee Hearty Fruit)*   0

Mulberries:
　fresh   0

Mullet:
striped:
raw, meat only, 4 oz. 56
raw, 1 fillet, 4.2 oz. (from 1½-lb. whole fish) 59
baked or broiled, meat only, 4 oz. 71
baked or broiled, 1 fillet, 3.3 oz. (4.2 oz. raw) 59

Mushroom:
all varieties, fresh or dried 0
all varieties, canned or frozen, without sauce 0

Mushroom gravy:
canned 0
dehydrated mix, prepared with water, 1 cup . . 1

Mushroom sauce mix:
dehydrated, 1-oz. packet 43
prepared with whole milk, 1 cup 34

Mussels:
blue:
raw, meat only, 4 oz. 32
raw, meat only, 1 cup or 5.3 oz. 42
boiled or steamed, meat only, 4 oz. 64

Mustard:
seeds or powder 0

Mustard, prepared:
all varieties 0

Mustard greens:
fresh or frozen 0

Mustard sauce:
hot *(Sauceworks)*, 1 tbsp.   5

Mustard spinach:
fresh   0

Mutton tallow, see "Tallow"

N

Food and Measure	Cholesterol (mgs.)

Natal plum, see "Carissa"

Natto, see "Soybean, fermented"

Nectarine:
fresh 0

New England Brand sausage:
beef and pork, 1 oz. 14
beef and pork, 1 slice, 4" diam. × 1/8" 11
(Oscar Mayer), .82-oz. slice 13

New Zealand spinach:
fresh 0

Noodle, Chinese:
canned *(Chun King)* 0
chow mein, canned, 1 cup 5

Noodle, egg:
regular or spinach *(Ronzoni)*, 2 oz. dry ...... < 86
cooked, 1 cup 50

Nutmeg:
whole or ground 0

Nutmeg butter:
raw or roasted 0

Nuts, see specific listings

Nuts, mixed:
all blends 0

Nuts and dried fruit:
all blends 0

O

The Cholesterol Content of Food

Food and Measure	Cholesterol (mgs.)

Oat bran:
crude or processed 0

Oats, see "Cereal, cooking" and "Cereal, ready-to-eat"

Ocean perch:
raw, meat only, 4 oz. 48
raw, 1 fillet, 2.3 oz. (from 1 lb. whole fish) 27
baked or broiled, meat only, 4 oz. 61
baked or broiled, 1 fillet, 1.8 oz. (2.3 oz. raw) 27

Octopus:
raw, meat only, 4 oz. 54

Oil:

all vegetable, grain, nut, and seed oils 0

Oil, fish, see specific listings

Okra:

fresh 0

frozen, without sauce 0

Old-fashioned cocktail:

fluid or mix 0

Old-fashioned loaf:

(Armour), 1 oz. 15

(Oscar Mayer), 1-oz. slice 14

Olive loaf:

(Armour), 1-oz. slice 10

(Oscar Mayer), 1-oz. slice 10

pork, 1-oz. slice 11

Olive oil, see "Oil"

Olives:

all varieties, fresh, cured, or pickled 0

Onion:

mature or green (scallion), fresh or dry 0

Onion, fried:

rings, frozen *(Ore-Ida)* 0

Onion, spiced:

cocktail, in jars *(Vlasic)* 0

Onion, Welsh:
  fresh 0

Onion dip:
  creamy *(Kraft* Premium), 1 oz. 10
  French *(Kraft)* 0
  French *(Kraft* Premium), 1 oz. 10
  French *(Nalley's)*, 1 oz. 14
  French *(Thank You)*, 2 tbsp. 1
  green *(Kraft)* 0

Onion gravy mix:
  dehydrated, prepared with water, 1 cup 1

Onion powder:
  plain or seasoned 0

Onion salt:
  plain or parslied 0

Orange:
  all varieties, fresh 0
  Mandarin, canned 0

Orange juice or drink:
  fresh, canned, dehydrated, frozen, or mix 0

Orange extract:
  (Virginia Dare) 0

Orange-grapefruit juice:
  canned or frozen 0

Orange Julius:
  raspberry cream supreme drink:
    small, 12 fl. oz. 55
    regular, 16 fl. oz. 80
    large, 20 fl. oz. 105
  tropical cream supreme drink:
    small, 12 fl. oz. 65
    regular, 16 fl. oz. 95
    large, 20 fl. oz. 115

Orange-pineapple juice:
  canned or frozen 0

Orange bar or roll:
  natural or sweetened 0

Oregano:
  fresh or dried 0

Oyster:
  eastern, fresh:
    raw, meat only, 4 oz. 62
    raw, meat only, 3 oz. (from 6 medium
      oysters) 46
    raw, meat only, 1 cup or 8.7 oz. 136
    steamed, meat only, 4 oz. 124
    steamed, meat only, 1.5 oz. (from 6 medium
      oysters) 46
  eastern, canned:
    with liquid, 4 oz. 62
    with liquid, 1 cup or 8.7 oz. 136
  European, raw, meat only, 4 oz. 34

Oyster stew, see "Soup, canned, condensed"

P

Food and Measure	Cholesterol (mgs.)

Pancake mix:
regular, prepared with egg, milk, and oil,
  4"-diam. cake 16
buckwheat, prepared with egg and milk,
  4"-diam. cake 20

Pancake syrup:
all blends, bottled 0

Pancreas, see "Pork pancreas"

Papaw:
fresh 0

Papaya:
fresh 0

Papaya nectar:
canned 0

Paprika:
hot or mild, ground 0

Parsley:
fresh, dried, or freeze-dried 0

Parsnips:
fresh 0

Passion fruit:
fresh 0

Passion fruit juice:
purple or yellow, fresh 0

Pasta:
all varieties (spaghetti, linguine, vermicelli, etc.),
   except egg pasta, dry or cooked 0
artichoke, Jerusalem, dry *(De Boles)* 0
corn, wheat-free, dry *(De Boles)* 0
whole wheat, organic, dry *(De Boles)* 0

Pastrami:
1-oz. slice 26
(Oscar Mayer), ¾-oz. slice 8
smoked *(Carl Buddig)*, 1 oz. 16
turkey, see "Turkey pastrami"

Pâté:
de foie gras, 1 oz. 43
de foie gras, 1 tbsp. 20

Pâté *(cont.)*

de foie gras, 1 tsp. 7

goose liver, smoked, 1 oz. 43

goose liver, smoked, 1 tbsp. 20

Pea pods, Chinese, see "Peas, snow"

Peach:

fresh, canned, dried, or frozen 0

Peach, spiced:

canned or in jars 0

Peach butter:

in jars 0

Peach drink or nectar:

canned or in jars 0

Peanut:

all varieties, raw, dried, roasted, or toasted . . . 0

Peanut butter:

fresh or in jars 0

Peanut flour:

defatted 0

Peanut oil, see "Oil"

Pear:

fresh, canned, dried, or frozen 0

Pear nectar:
canned   0

Peas, green:
fresh or canned   0
frozen, without sauce   0

Peas, mature seeds:
dry, whole, or split   0

Peas, snow:
fresh or frozen   0

Peas and carrots:
fresh or canned   0
frozen, without sauce   0

Pecans:
raw, dried, or roasted   0

Pepper:
seasoning, all varieties, whole or ground   0

Pepper, banana or cherry:
mild or hot, canned or in jars   0

Pepper, chili:
green and red, fresh, dried, canned, or in jars   0

Pepper, green and red, see "Pepper, chili" and "Pepper, sweet"

Pepper, green, stuffed, dinner:
frozen *(Dinner Classics)*, 12 oz.   70

Pepper, jalapeño:
fresh, canned, or in jars 0

Pepper, sweet:
all varieties, fresh or frozen 0

Pepper sauce:
hot or mild 0

Peppered loaf:
(Oscar Mayer), 1-oz. slice 13
pork and beef, 1-oz. slice 13

Pepperoncini:
canned or in jars 0

Pepperoni:
sliced or Italian style *(Armour)*, 1 oz. 20

Perch:
mixed species:
   raw, meat only, 4 oz. 102
   raw, 1 fillet, 2.1 oz. (from 3/4 lb. whole fish) 76
   baked or broiled, meat only, 4 oz. 130
   baked or broiled, 1 fillet, 1.6 oz. (2.1 oz. raw) 53
ocean, see "Ocean perch"
white, raw, meat only, 4 oz. 91
yellow, raw, meat only, 4 oz. 102

Persimmon:
native, Japanese (kaki), fresh 0

Pheasant:
raw, meat only, 4 oz. 75

Picante sauce:
  all varieties, canned or in jars   0

Pickle:
  all varieties, fresh or in jars   0

Pickle and pimiento loaf:
  (Armour), 1-oz. slice   10
  (Oscar Mayer), 1-oz. slice   12
  pork, 1-oz. slice   10

Pickle relish:
  all varieties, fresh or in jars   0

Picnic loaf:
  (Oscar Mayer), 1-oz. slice   12
  pork and beef, 1-oz. slice   11

Pie* :
  apple, blueberry, cherry, or peach, without
    cream   0
  cream, 1/6 of 9"-diam. pie   8
  custard, 1/6 of 9"-diam. pie   169
  lemon meringue, 1/6 of 9"-diam. pie   143
  pecan, 1/6 of 9"-diam. pie   95
  pumpkin, 1/6 of 9"-diam. pie   109

Pie, snack:
  apple *(Hostess)*, 1 pie   18
  apple, fried, 3-oz. pie   14
  berry *(Hostess)*, 1 pie   18
  blueberry *(Hostess)*, 1 pie   18

---
* Pie crust made with vegetable shortening

Pie, snack *(cont.)*
cherry *(Hostess)*, 1 pie . . . .　18
cherry, fried, 3-oz. pie . . . .　13
lemon *(Hostess)*, 1 pie . . . .　30
peach *(Hostess)*, 1 pie . . . .　18
strawberry *(Hostess)*, 1 pie . . . .　13

Pie crust mix:
prepared with vegetable shortening . . . .　0

Pie filling:
fruit, chocolate, coconut, mincemeat, or
　pumpkin, canned . . . .　0

Pierogies:
frozen *(Golden)*, 1 piece . . . .　4

Pigeon, see "Squab"

Pigeon peas:
raw or dried . . . .　0

Pig's feet:
fresh, braised, meat only, 2 oz. . . . .　57
pickled, meat only, 2 oz. . . . .　52

Pignolias, see "Pine nuts"

Pike:
northern:
　raw, meat only, 4 oz. . . . .　44
　raw, 1/2 fillet, 7 oz. (from 5-lb. whole fish) . .　77
　baked or broiled, meat only, 4 oz. . . . .　57
　baked or broiled, 1/2 fillet, 5.5 oz. (7 oz. raw)　78

Pike *(cont.)*
  walleye:
    raw, meat only, 4 oz.   98
    raw, 1 fillet, 5.6 oz. (from 2-lb. whole fish) . .   137

Pili nuts:
  raw or dried   0

Pimiento:
  canned or in jars   0

Piña colada cocktail:
  fluid or mix   0

Pineapple:
  fresh, canned, dried, or frozen   0

Pineapple juice:
  fresh, canned, or frozen   0

Pineapple-grapefruit juice:
  canned or frozen   0

Pineapple-orange juice:
  canned or frozen   0

Pine nuts:
  pignolias or pinons, raw or dried   0

Pistachio nuts:
  red or white, dried or roasted   0

Pitanga:
  fresh   0

Pizza, see "*Domino's Pizza*" and "*Godfather's Pizza*

Pizza sauce:
chunky *(Ragu Pizza Quick)*   0

Plaice:
European, raw, meat only, 4 oz.   79

Plantain:
fresh   0

Plum:
fresh or canned   0

Poi:
prepared   0

Poke shoots:
raw   0

Pokeberry, see "Poke shoots"

Polish sausage:
kielbasa:
    beef *(Hillshire Farm)*, 3½ oz.   29
    endless *(Hillshire Farm)*, 3½ oz.   23
    pork and beef, 1 oz.   19
    pork and beef, 1 slice, 6" × 3¾" × 1/16"   17
  pork, 8-oz. sausage, 10" long × 1¼" diam. . .   158
  pork, 1 oz.   20

Pollack:
  Atlantic:
    raw, meat only, 4 oz.   81
    raw, 1/2 fillet, 6.8 oz. (from 5-lb. whole fish)   136
  walleye:
    raw, meat only, 4 oz.   81
    raw, 1 fillet, 2.7 oz. (from 1-lb. whole fish) . .   55
    baked or broiled, meat only, 4 oz.   109
    baked or broiled, 1 fillet, 2.1 oz. (2.7 oz. raw)   58

Pomegranate:
  fresh   0

Pomegranate juice:
  fresh or bottled   0

Pompano:
  Florida:
    raw, meat only, 4 oz.   57
    raw, 1 fillet, 3.9 oz. (from 1 1/2-lb. whole fish)   56
    baked or broiled, meat only, 4 oz.   73
    baked or broiled, 1 fillet, 3.1 oz. (3.9 oz. raw)   56

Popcorn:
  plain or with oil   0

Poppy seed:
  dried   0

Poppy seed oil, see "Oil"

Pork, fresh, edible portions:
  Boston blade (shoulder), lean with separable
      fat:
    braised, 4 oz.   126

Pork, Boston blade (shoulder), lean with separable
fat *(cont.)*

    braised, 5.6 oz. (from 6.3-oz. steak with
        bone) 178

    broiled, 4 oz. 117

    broiled, 6.5 oz. (from 7.4-oz. steak with bone) 190

    roasted, 4 oz. 110

    roasted, 6.5 oz. (from 7.5-oz. steak with
        bone) 179

  Boston blade (shoulder), lean only (fat
    trimmed):

    braised, 4 oz. 132

    braised, 4.6 oz. (6.3-oz. steak with bone and
        fat) 151

    broiled, 4 oz. 119

    broiled, 5.3 oz. (7.4-oz. steak with bone and
        fat) 159

    roasted, 4 oz. 111

    roasted, 5.6 oz. (7.5-oz. steak with bone and
        fat) 155

  center loin, lean with separable fat:

    braised, 4 oz. 121

    braised, 2.6 oz. (from 3.2-oz. chop with
        bone) 81

    broiled, 4 oz. 110

    broiled, 3.1 oz. (from 3.7-oz. chop with bone) 84

    pan-fried, 4 oz. 117

    pan-fried, 3.1 oz. (from 4-oz. chop with bone) 92

    roasted, 4 oz. 103

    roasted, 3.1 oz. (from 3.8-oz. chop with
        bone) 80

  center loin, lean only (fat trimmed):

    braised, 4 oz. 126

Pork, center loin, lean only (fat trimmed) *(cont.)*

braised, 2.2 oz. (3.2-oz. chop with bone and fat)	68
broiled, 4 oz.	111
broiled, 2.5 oz. (3.7-oz. chop with bone and fat)	71
pan-fried, 4 oz.	121
pan-fried, 2.4 oz. (4-oz. chop with bone and fat)	71
roasted, 4 oz.	103
roasted, 2.5 oz. (3.8-oz. chop with bone and fat)	68
center rib, lean with separable fat:	
braised, 4 oz.	108
braised, 2.4 oz. (from 3.1-oz. chop with bone)	64
broiled, 4 oz.	105
broiled, 2.7 oz. (from 3.7-oz. chop with bone)	72
pan-fried, 4 oz.	95
pan-fried, 3.1 oz. (from 4.2-oz. chop with bone)	74
roasted, 4 oz.	92
roasted, 2.8 oz. (from 3.8-oz. chop with bone)	64
center rib, lean only (fat trimmed):	
braised, 4 oz.	110
braised, 1.9 oz. (3.1-oz. chop with bone and fat)	51
broiled, 4 oz.	107
broiled, 2.2 oz. (3.7-oz. chop with bone and fat)	59
pan-fried, 4 oz.	92
pan-fried, 2.2 oz. (4.2-oz. chop with bone and fat)	50

Pork, center rib, lean only (fat trimmed) *(cont.)*

roasted, 4 oz.	90
roasted, 2.3 oz. (3.8-oz. chop with bone and fat)	52
leg, see "Ham"	
loin, blade, lean with separable fat:	
braised, 4 oz.	122
braised, 2.4 oz. (from 3.1-oz. chop with bone)	72
broiled, 4 oz.	111
broiled, 2.1 oz. (from 3.7-oz. chop with bone)	75
pan-fried, 4 oz.	108
pan-fried, 3.1 oz. (from 4.3-oz. chop with bone)	85
roasted, 4 oz.	102
roasted, 3.1 oz. (from 4.2-oz. chop with bone)	79
loin, blade, lean only (fat trimmed):	
braised, 4 oz.	128
braised, 1.8 oz. (3.1-oz. chop with bone and fat)	57
broiled, 4 oz.	113
broiled, 2.1 oz. (3.7-oz. chop with bone and fat)	59
pan-fried, 4 oz.	110
pan-fried, 3.1 oz. (4.3-oz. chop with bone and fat)	60
roasted, 4 oz.	101
roasted, 3.1 oz. (4.2-oz. chop with bone and fat)	63
loin, whole, lean with separable fat:	
braised, 4 oz.	116
braised, 2.5 oz. (from 3.1-oz. chop with bone)	73

Pork, loin, whole, lean with separable fat *(cont.)*
    broiled, 4 oz. 107
    broiled, 2.9 oz. (from 3.7-oz. chop with bone) 77
    roasted, 4 oz. 102
    roasted, 2.9 oz. (from 3.7-oz. chop with
      bone) 74
  loin, whole, lean only (fat trimmed):
    braised, 4 oz. 119
    braised, 1.9 oz. (3.1-oz. chop with bone and
      fat) 58
    broiled, 4 oz. 108
    broiled, 2.3 oz. (3.7-oz. chop with bone and
      fat) 63
    roasted, 4 oz. 102
    roasted, 2.4 oz. (3.7-oz. chop with bone and
      fat) 62
  picnic (shoulder), lean with separable fat:
    braised, 4 oz. 124
    braised, chopped or diced, 1 cup 153
    roasted, 4 oz. 107
    roasted, chopped or diced, 1 cup 132
  picnic (shoulder), lean only (fat trimmed):
    braised, 4 oz. 129
    braised, chopped or diced, 1 cup 160
    roasted, 4 oz. 108
    roasted, chopped or diced, 1 cup 133
  shoulder, whole, lean with separable fat:
    roasted, 4 oz. 109
    roasted, chopped or diced, 1 cup 134
  shoulder, whole, lean only (fat trimmed):
    roasted, 4 oz. 110
    roasted, chopped or diced, 1 cup 135
  sirloin, lean with separable fat:
    braised, 4 oz. 120

Pork, sirloin, lean with separable fat *(cont.)*

braised, 2.5 oz. (from 3.1-oz. chop with
bone) 75

broiled, 4 oz. 110

broiled, 3 oz. (from 3.7-oz. chop with bone) 81

roasted, 4 oz. 103

roasted, 3 oz. (from 3.8-oz. chop with bone) 76

sirloin, lean only (fat trimmed):

braised, 4 oz. 125

braised, 2 oz. (3.1-oz. chop with bone and
fat) 63

broiled, 4 oz. 111

broiled, 2.4 oz. (3.7-oz. chop with bone and
fat) 67

roasted, 4 oz. 102

roasted, 2.6 oz. (3.8-oz. chop with bone and
fat) 67

spareribs, lean with separable fat:

braised, 4 oz. 137

braised, 6.3 oz. (yield from 1 lb. raw with
bone) 214

tenderloin, lean only (fat trimmed):

roasted, 4 oz. 105

roasted, 12.4 oz. (yield from 1 lb. raw,
boneless) 333

top loin, lean with separable fat:

braised, 4 oz. 108

braised, 2.5 oz. (from 3.1-oz. chop with
bone) 67

broiled, 4 oz. 105

broiled, 2.9 oz. (from 3.7-oz. chop with bone) 76

pan-fried, 4 oz. 95

pan-fried, 3 oz. (from 4.1-oz. chop with bone) 72

roasted, 4 oz. 93

Pork, top loin, lean with separable fat *(cont.)*
   roasted, 2.9 oz. (from 3.8-oz. chop with
    bone) 68
  top loin, lean only (fat trimmed):
   braised, 4 oz. 110
   braised, 1.9 oz. (3.1-oz. chop with bone and
    fat) 51
   broiled, 4 oz. 107
   broiled, 2.3 oz. (3.7-oz. chop with bone and
    fat) 60
   pan-fried, 4 oz. 92
   pan-fried, 2.2 oz. (4.1-oz. chop with bone
    and fat) 49
   roasted, 4 oz. 90
   roasted, 2.4 oz. (3.8-oz. chop with bone and
    fat) 54

Pork, cured, see "Ham" and specific listings

Pork, salt:
  raw, 1 oz. 212

Pork backfat:
  raw, 1 oz. 16

Pork brains, see "Brains"

Pork chitterlings:
  braised or simmered, 4 oz. 162

Pork dinner, sweet and sour:
  frozen *(Dinner Classics),* 12 oz. 95

Pork entrée:

chow mein, canned, drained *(Chun King* Stir-Fry), 6 oz. 23

sweet and sour, frozen *(Chun King* Boil-in-Bag), 10 oz. 43

Pork gravy mix:

dehydrated, prepared with water, 1 cup 3

Pork lard:

8 oz. 215

1 cup 195

1 tbsp. 12

Pork liver, see "Liver"

Pork pancreas:

fresh, raw, 4 oz. 218

fresh, braised or simmered, 4 oz. 357

Pork stomach:

raw, 4 oz. 218

Potato:

fresh or canned 0

frozen:

without sauce 0

fried or frying, all varieties, except cheese *(Ore-Ida)* 0

fried, with cheese *(Ore-Ida Cheedar Browns),* 3 oz. 10

hashed brown, with butter sauce, 3.5 oz. . . . 23

dehydrated 0

granules or flakes, with dry milk solids, 1/2 cup 2

Potato, sweet, see "Sweet potato"

Potato chips:
  plain or barbecue flavor   0
  au gratin cheese flavor *(O'Grady's)*, 1 oz. . . . .   tr.
  bacon and sour cream flavor *(Ruffles)*   0
  sour cream and onion flavor:
    (Bachman)   0
    (Laura Scudder's)   0
    (Lay's), 1 1/8 oz. . . . .   tr.
    (Ruffles), 1 oz. . . . .   tr.

Potato pancake:
  frozen *(Golden)*, 1 piece   7

Potato salad:
  prepared with mayonnaise, 1/2 cup   85

Potato starch:
  (Manischewitz)   0

Potato sticks:
  fresh, canned, or packaged   0

Potatoes au gratin:
  prepared from dry mix*, 1 cup   12

Potatoes, mashed:
  deydrated, prepared with whole milk and butter,
    1/2 cup   15
  granules, prepared with whole milk and butter,
    1/2 cup   18

---

* *Prepared according to package directions*

Potatoes, scalloped:
   prepared from dry mix*, 1 cup   27

Poultry, see specific listings

Poultry salad, sandwich spread:
   chicken and turkey, 1 oz.   9
   chicken and turkey, 1 tbsp.   4

Pout:
   ocean:
      raw, meat only, 4 oz.   60
      raw, 1/2 fillet, 6.2 oz. (from 5-lb. whole fish)   92

Preserves, see "Jams and preserves"

Pretzels:
   all varieties *(Bachman)*   0
   all varieties *(Laura Scudder's)*   0
   all varieties *(Rold Gold)*   0
   all varieties *(Quinlan)*, 1 oz.   1
   (A & Eagle)   0
   hard *(Snyders)*   0
   sticks or thins *(Snyders)*, 1 oz.   1

Prickly pear:
   fresh   0

Prune:
   canned, dehydrated, or dried   0

---

* *Prepared according to package directions*

Prune juice:
  canned or in jars   0

Pudding, ready-to-serve:
  banana *(Thank You)*, 1/2 cup.   1
  butterscotch *(Thank You)*, 1/2 cup   1
  chocolate or chocolate fudge *(Thank You)*, 1/2
    cup   1
  custard, egg *(Thank You)*, 1/2 cup   70
  lemon *(Thank You)*, 1/2 cup   11
  rice *(Thank You)*, 1/2 cup   1
  tapioca *(Thank You)*, 1/2 cup   1
  vanilla *(Thank You)*, 1/2 cup   1

Pudding, mix* :
  chocolate, instant, 1/2 cup   14
  chocolate, regular, 1/2 cup   15
  rice, 1/2 cup   15
  tapioca, 1/2 cup   15
  vanilla, instant or regular, 1/2 cup   15

Pummelo:
  fresh.   0

Pumpkin:
  fresh or canned   0

Pumpkin flowers:
  fresh.   0

Pumpkin pie filling, see "Pie filling"

----
* Prepared according to package directions, with whole milk

Pumpkin seed kernels:
fresh or dried 0

Purple granadilla, see "Passion fruit"

Purslane:
fresh 0

Q

Quail:
raw, meat only, 4 oz.   79

Queensland nuts, see "Macadamia nuts"

Quiche:
bacon and onion *(Pour-A-Quiche)*, 4 1/3 oz. . . .   240
ham *(Pour-A-Quiche)*, 4 1/3 oz.   235
spinach and onion *(Pour-A-Quiche)*, 4 1/3 oz. . .   230
three cheese *(Pour-A-Quiche)*, 4 1/3 oz.   250

Quince:
fresh   0

R

Food and Measure	Cholesterol (mgs.)
Rabbit:	
wild, raw, meat only, 4 oz.	74
Radish:	
all varieties, fresh or dried	0
Radish seeds:	
raw	0
Raisins:	
all varieties	0
Ranch house dip:	
(Nalley's), 1 oz.	17

Raspberries:
  fresh, canned, or frozen 0

Raspberry danish:
  (Hostess), 1 danish 20

Raspberry juice:
  canned or bottled 0

Raspberry-cranberry drink:
  canned or bottled 0

Raspberry roll or bar:
  natural or sweetened 0

Ravioli:
  beef, canned *(Nalley's)*, 3½ oz. 5
  cheese, round, canned *(Buitoni)*, 4 oz. 25
  cheese, square, canned *(Buitoni)*, 4 oz. 95
  meat, square, canned *(Buitoni)*, 4 oz. 35

Red and gray snapper, see "Snapper"

Redfish, see "Perch, ocean"

Relish, see "Pickle relish"

Rennet tablets:
  (Junket) 0

Rhubarb:
  fresh 0
  frozen, sweetened or unsweetened 0

Rice:
  all varieties, dry 0

Rice, frozen:
  Chinese fried *(Birds Eye)* 0
  Chinese fried, with pork *(Chun King* Boil-in-
    Bag), 10 oz. 74
  French, Italian, or Spanish style *(Birds Eye)* . . 0
  with peas and mushrooms *(Birds Eye)* 0

Rice cake:
  all varieties *(Chico-San)* 0

Rice pilaf mix:
  all varieties, dry *(Casbah)* 0

Rice, wild:
  raw 0

Rice bran:
  crude or processed 0

Rockfish:
  Pacific, mixed species:
    raw, meat only, 4 oz. 40
    raw, 1 fillet, 6.7 oz. (from 3-lb. whole fish) . . 66
    baked or broiled, meat only, 4 oz. 50
    baked or broiled, 1 fillet, 5.3 oz. (6.7 oz. raw) 66

Roe (see also "Caviar"):
  mixed species, raw, 1 oz. 105

Roll:
  biscuit, see "Biscuit"

Roll *(cont.)*
  brown and serve:
    (Roman Meal) 0
    (Wonder Half & Half/Home Bake), 1 roll . . . < 5
    with buttermilk *(Wonder)*, 1 roll . . . . < 5
    gem style *(Wonder)*, 1 roll . . . . < 5
  croissant, see "Croissant"
  dinner:
    (Home Pride), 1 roll . . . . < 5
    (Roman Meal) 0
    (Wonder), 1 roll . . . . < 5
  hamburger or hot dog:
    (Freihofer's New England Frankfurter Roll), 1
      roll . . . . < 5
    (Roman Meal) 0
    (Wonder), 1 roll . . . . < 5
  hoagie *(Wonder)*, 1 roll . . . . < 5
  sandwich *(Freihofer's* Mates), 1 roll . . . . < 5

Roseapple:
  fresh 0

Roselle:
  fresh 0

Rosemary:
  fresh or dried 0

Roughy:
  orange, raw, meat only, 4 oz. 23

Roy Rogers:
  breakfast, 1 serving:
    crescent roll, 2.5-oz. roll . . . . < 5

Roy Rogers, breakfast, 1 serving *(cont.)*

crescent sandwich, 4.5 oz.	148
with bacon, 4.75 oz.	156
with ham, 5.9 oz.	189
with sausage, 5.8 oz.	168
egg and biscuit platter, 5.9 oz.	284
with bacon, 6.2 oz.	294
with ham, 7.15 oz.	304
with sausage, 7.25 oz.	325
pancake platter, 5.9 oz.	53
with bacon, 6.2 oz.	63
with ham, 7.15 oz.	73
with sausage, 7.25 oz.	94

chicken, fried:

breast, 5.15-oz. piece	118
breast and wing, 7-oz. serving	165
leg (drumstick), 1.9-oz. piece	40
thigh, 3.5-oz. piece	85
thigh and leg, 5.4-oz. serving	125
wing, 1.87-oz. piece	47

sandwiches, 1 serving:

bacon cheeseburger, 6.4 oz.	103
bar burger, 7.43 oz.	115
cheeseburger, 6.2 oz.	95
hamburger, 5.1 oz.	73
roast beef, 5.5 oz.	55
roast beef, large, 6.5 oz.	73
roast beef with cheese, 6.5 oz.	77
roast beef with cheese, large, 7.5 oz.	95

hot top potatoes, 1 serving:

plain	0
with oleo	0
with sour cream and chives, 10.6 oz.	31
with bacon 'n cheese, 8.8 oz.	34

Roy Rogers, hot top potatoes, 1 serving *(cont.)*

    with broccoli 'n cheese, 11.1 oz. . . . . < 19

    with taco beef 'n cheese, 12.8 oz.   37

  side dishes, 1 serving:

    biscuit, 2.25 oz. < 5

    cole slaw, 3.5 oz. . . . . < 5

    French fries, 3 oz.   42

    French fries, large, 4 oz.   56

    macaroni salad, 3.5 oz. . . . . < 5

    potato salad, 3.5 oz. . . . . < 5

  desserts and shakes:

    brownie, 2.3 oz.   10

    danish, apple, 2.53 oz.   15

    danish, cheese, 2.53 oz.   11

    danish, cherry, 2.53 oz.   11

    shake, chocolate, 1 shake   37

    shake, strawberry, 1 shake   37

    shake, vanilla, 1 shake   40

    strawberry shortcake, 7.3 oz.   28

    sundae, caramel, 5.2 oz.   23

    sundae, hot fudge, 5.4 oz.   23

    sundae, strawberry, 5 oz.   23

Rum, see "Liquor"

Rutabaga:

  fresh or frozen   0

Rye whiskey, see "Liquor"

S

The Cholesterol Content of Food   174

Food and Measure	Cholesterol (mgs.)

Sablefish:
  fresh:
    raw, meat only, 4 oz. 56
    raw, 1/2 fillet, 6.8 oz. (from 5-lb. whole fish)   95
  smoked, 4 oz. 73

Safflower oil, see "Oil"

Safflower seed kernels:
  raw or dried 0

Safflower seed meal:
  partially defatted 0

Saffron:
  whole or ground 0

Sage:
fresh or dried   0

Salad dressing, bottled:
(A&P/P&Q), 1 tbsp.   8
(Miracle Whip), 1 tbsp.   5
(Mrs. Filbert's), 1 tbsp.   5
bacon, creamy (Kraft Reduced Calorie)   0
bacon and buttermilk (Kraft)   0
bacon and tomato (Kraft/Kraft Reduced
  Calorie)   0
blue cheese:
  (Roka Brand), 1 tbsp.   10
  (Roka Brand Reduced Calorie), 1 tbsp.   5
  chunky (Kraft/Kraft Reduced Calorie)   0
  chunky (Wish-Bone/Wish-Bone Lite), 1 tbsp.   tr.
blue cheese and bacon (Philadelphia Brand) . .   0
buttermilk:
  (Wish-Bone Lite), 1 tbsp. . . . .   tr.
  creamy (Kraft), 1 tbsp.   5
  creamy (Kraft Reduced Calorie)   0
buttermilk and chives, creamy (Kraft), 1 tbsp.   5
Caesar:
  (Bernstein Extra Rich), 1 tbsp.   5
  (Wish Bone), 1 tbsp. . . . .   tr.
  golden (Kraft)   0
coleslaw (Kraft), 1 tbsp.   10
cucumber:
  creamy (Kraft/Kraft Reduced Calorie)   0
  creamy (Wish-Bone), 1 tbsp. . . . .   tr.
  creamy (Wish-Bone Lite)   0
Cheddar and bacon (Wish Bone), 1 tbsp. . . . .   tr.
French:
  (Catalina Brand)   0

Salad dressing, French *(cont.)*

    (Kraft/Kraft Reduced Calorie) 0

    (Wish-Bone Deluxe/Lite French Style) 0

    garlic, herbal or sweet 'n spicy *(Wish-Bone)* 0

    low-calorie, 1 tbsp. 1

garlic, creamy *(Wish-Bone)* 0

garlic and chives *(Philadelphia Brand)* 0

garlic and oil *(Hain Naturals)* 0

Italian:

    (Bernstein Restaurant Recipe), 1 tbsp. . . . . < 1

    (Kraft Reduced Calorie/Zesty) 0

    (Wish-Bone/Wish-Bone Lite/Robusto) 0

    with cheese *(Bernstein)*, 1 tbsp. . . . . < 1

    with cheese and garlic *(Bernstein)*, 1 tbsp. . . < 1

    creamy *(Kraft* Reduced Calorie) 0

    creamy *(Wish Bone/Wish Bone* Lite) 0

    creamy, with sour cream *(Kraft)* 0

    herb *(Philadelphia Brand)* 0

    herbal *(Wish-Bone)* 0

    low-calorie, 1 tbsp. 1

    oil free *(Kraft)* 0

mayonnaise, see "Mayonnaise"

mayonnaise-type, 1 tbsp. 4

oil & vinegar *(Kraft)* 0

onion 'n chive *(Wish-Bone)* 0

onion and chive, creamy *(Kraft)* 0

Roquefort *(Bernstein)*, 1 tbsp. 11

Russian:

    (Kraft/Kraft Reduced Calorie) 0

    (Wish-Bone/Wish-Bone Lite) 0

    low-calorie, 1 tbsp. 1

sesame seed 0

sour cream and bacon *(Wish-Bone)*, 1 tbsp. . . tr.

Salad dressing *(cont.)*
Thousand Island:
(Bernstein), 1 tbsp. 9
(Kraft/Kraft Reduced Calorie), 1 tbsp. 5
(Nalley's), 1 tbsp. 8
(Wish-Bone), 1 tbsp. 5
(Wish-Bone Lite/Southern Recipe), 1 tbsp.   10
and bacon (Kraft) 0
with bacon (Wish-Bone Southern Recipe), 1
    tbsp. 5
low-calorie, 1 tbsp. 2

Salad sprinkles:
(Lawry's) 0

Salami:
beer (beerwurst):
(Oscar Mayer), .82-oz. slice 15
beef (Oscar Mayer), .82-oz. slice 15
pork, 1 slice, 4″ diam. × 1/8″ 13
pork, 1 slice, 2³/4″ diam. × 1/16″ 4
cooked (Armour), 1 oz. 20
cotto (cooked):
(Oscar Mayer), .82-oz. slice 15
beef, 1 oz. 17
beef, 1 slice (10 per 8-oz. pkg.) 14
beef (Oscar Mayer), .82-oz. slice 15
beef and pork, 1 oz. 18
beef and pork, 1 slice (10 per 8-oz. pkg.) . . 15
Genoa:
(Armour), 1-oz. slice 30
(Oscar Mayer), 1/3-oz. slice 8
hard or dry:
4-oz. pkg. 89

Salami, hard or dry *(cont.)*
  1 slice (12 per 4-oz. pkg.) 8
  (Armour), 1 oz. 20
  (Oscar Mayer), 1/3-oz. slice 7
  Italian *(Armour),* 1 oz. 20
  turkey, see "Turkey salami"

Salisbury steak dinner, frozen:
  (Classic Lite), 10 oz. 75
  (Dinner Classics), 11 oz. 105
  (Lean Cuisine), 9 1/2 oz. 95

Salmon:
  Atlantic:
    raw, meat only, 4 oz. 62
    raw, 1/2 fillet, 7 oz. (from 5 lb. whole fish) . . 109
    blueback, canned *(Gill Netters Best),* 3.5 oz. 62
  Chinook, fresh:
    raw, meat only, 4 oz. 75
    raw, 1/2 fillet, 7 oz. (from 5-lb. whole fish) . . 131
  Chinook, smoked, meat only, 4 oz. 26
  chum, fresh:
    raw, meat only, 4 oz. 84
    raw, 1/2 fillet, 7 oz. (from 5-lb. whole fish) . . 147
  chum, canned:
    (Humpty-Dumpty), 3.5 oz. 62
    drained solids, 13-oz. can 144
    drained solids, 4 oz. 44
  coho:
    raw, meat only, 4 oz. 44
    raw, 1/2 fillet, 7 oz. (from 5-lb. whole fish) . . 77
    poached or steamed, meat only, 4 oz. 56
    poached or steamed, 1/2 fillet, 5.5 oz. (7 oz.
      raw) 76

Salmon *(cont.)*
  pink, fresh:
    raw, meat only, 4 oz.   59
    raw, 1/2 fillet, 5.6 oz. (from 4-lb. whole fish)   83
  pink, Alaska, canned *(Double "Q")*, 3.5 oz. . . .   62
  smoked, see "Chinook," above
  sockeye (red), fresh:
    raw, meat only, 4 oz.   70
    raw, 1/2 fillet, 7 oz. (from 5-lb. whole fish) . .   123
    baked or broiled, meat only, 4 oz.   99
    baked or broiled, 1/2 fillet, 5.5 oz. (7 oz. raw)   135
  sockeye (red), canned:
    (Demings/Peter Pan), 3.5 oz.   62
    drained solids, 13-oz. can   161
    drained solids, 4 oz.   50

Salmon oil:
  1 oz.   137

Salsa:
  all varieties, canned or in jars   0

Salsify:
  fresh   0

Salt:
  table, regular or seasoned   0

Salt pork, see "Pork, salt"

Sandwich spread (see also specific listings):
  1/2 cup   94
  1 tbsp.   12
  (Best Foods/Hellmann's), 1 tbsp.   5

Sandwich spread *(cont.)*
(Kraft), 1 tbsp. 5
(Oscar Mayer), 1 oz. 10
pork and beef, 1 oz. 11
pork and beef, 1 tbsp. 6

Sapodilla:
fresh 0

Sapote:
fresh 0

Sardine:
Atlantic, canned in oil, drained:
3.2-oz. can 131
4 oz. 161
2 sardines (3″ × 1″ × 1/2″), .8 oz. 34
Pacific, canned in tomato sauce, drained:
13-oz. can 225
4 oz. 69
1 sardine (43/4″ × 11/8″ × 5/8″), 1.3 oz. . . . 23

Sauces, see specific listings

Sauerkraut:
canned or in jars 0

Sauerkraut juice:
canned or bottled 0

Sausage, links and patties (see also specific
listings):
blood, see "Blood sausage"

Sausage *(cont.)*

brown and serve:

beef *(Swift Original Brown 'N Serve)*, 2 links — 25

pork *(Swift Original Brown 'N Serve)*, 2 links — 30

pork *(Swift Brown 'N Serve Country Recipe)*, 2 links . . . . — 35

pork *(Swift Original Brown 'N Serve)*, 2 patties . . . . — 40

Italian:

raw, 1 link (4 per lb.) . . . . — 86

raw, 1 link (5 per lb.) . . . . — 69

cooked, 1 link (4 per lb. raw) . . . . — 65

cooked, 1 link (5 per lb. raw) . . . . — 52

hot *(Hillshire Farm)*, 3½ oz. . . . . — 37

mild *(Hillshire Farm)*, 3½ oz. . . . . — 26

kielbasa and Polish, see "Polish sausage"

luncheon, see "Luncheon meat"

pork:

raw, 1-oz. link . . . . — 19

raw, 2-oz. patty . . . . — 39

cooked, 1 link (1 oz. raw) . . . . — 11

cooked, 1 patty (2 oz. raw) . . . . — 22

cooked *(Oscar Mayer Little Friers)*, ¾-oz. link . . . . — 16

cooked, country style, 1 link, 4" × ⅞" . . . . — 11

cooked, country style, 1 patty, 3⅞" diam. × ¼" raw . . . . — 22

smoked:

(Hillshire Farm Endless), 3½ oz. . . . . — 20

(Hillshire Farms Links), 3½ oz. . . . . — 20

(Oscar Mayer Little Smokies), ⅓-oz. link . . . — 6

(Oscar Mayer Smokie Links), 1.5-oz. link . . . — 27

beef *(Hillshire Farm)*, 3½ oz. . . . . — 29

beef *(Oscar Mayer Smokies)*, 1.5-oz. link . . . — 27

Sausage, smoked *(cont.)*

    cheese *(Oscar Mayer* Smokies), 1.5-oz. link   28

    pork, grilled, 1 link, 4″ × 1⅛″ diam.   46

    pork, grilled, small, 1 link, 2″ × ¾″ diam. . .   11

    pork and beef, 1 link, 4″ × 1⅛″ diam.   48

    pork and beef, small, 1 link, 2″ × ¾″ diam.   11

    pork and beef, nonfat dry milk added, 4″ link   44

    pork and beef, nonfat dry milk added, 2″ link   10

    turkey, see "Turkey sausage"

    Vienna, canned, beef and pork, 7 links   59

    Vienna, canned, beef and pork, 1 link, 2″ ×

    ⅞″ diam.   8

Savory:

    ground   0

Scad:

    Muroaji, raw, meat only, 4 oz.   53

    other varieties, raw, meat only, 4 oz.   31

Scallion, see "Onion"

Scallop:

    bay and sea:

        raw, meat only, 4 oz.   37

        raw, 2 large or 5 small, meat only, 1.1 oz. . . .   10

Scallop, imitation:

    made from surimi, 4 oz.   25

Scallop Oriental dinner:

    frozen *(Lean Cuisine),* 11 oz.   20

Scotch whiskey, see "Liquor"

Scrod, see "Cod, Atlantic"

Screwdriver cocktail:
    fluid or mix   0

Sea bass:
    mixed species:
        raw, meat only, 4 oz.   46
        raw, 1 fillet, 4.6 oz. (from 1½-lb. whole fish)   53
        baked or broiled, meat only, 4 oz.   60
        baked or broiled, 1 fillet, 3.6 oz. (4.6 oz. raw)   53

Seafood, see specific listings

Seafood dinner, frozen:
    natural herbs *(Classic Lite)*, 11½ oz.   20
    Newburg *(Dinner Classics)*, 10½ oz.   65

Seasoned coating mix:
    for chicken or pork *(Shake 'n Bake)*   0

Seasoning, see specific listings

Seasoning, salt-free:
    (Lawry's)   0

Seasonings, see specific listings

Sea trout:
    mixed species:
        raw, meat only, 4 oz.   94
        raw, 1 fillet, 8.4 oz. (from 3-lb. whole fish) . .   198

Seaweed:
all varieties, fresh or dried 0

Sesame butter:
raw, unsalted *(Hain)* 0

Sesame paste:
raw, roasted, or toasted 0
tahini, canned or in jars 0

Sesame seed oil, see "Oil"

Sesame seeds:
raw or dried 0

Sesame snacks:
all varieties 0

Sesbania flower:
fresh 0

Shallot:
fresh or freeze-dried 0

Shake, fast-food (see also specific restaurant):
chocolate, 10 fl. oz. 37
strawberry, 10 fl. oz. 31
vanilla, 10 fl. oz. 32

Shark:
mixed species, raw, meat only, 4 oz. 58

Sheanut oil, see "Oil"

Sherbet:
all flavors, about 2% fat, 1/2 cup   7
all fruit flavors (*Dole* Fruit Sorbet)   0
all fruit flavors (*Land O Lakes*), 1/2 cup   5
all fruit flavors (*Shamitoff's* Sorbet)   0
chocolate coconut (*Shamitoff's* Sorbet)   0

Sherbet bar:
chocolate fudge (*Eskimo*)   0

Shortening:
lard, see "Pork lard"
soybean, cottonseed, palm, or vegetable   0
(*Crisco/Crisco* Butter Flavor   0
(*Snowdrift*)   0

Shrimp:
Atlantic:
brown, raw, meat only, 4 oz.   161
white, raw, meat only, 4 oz.   206
Japanese (kuruma) prawn, raw, meat only, 4
oz.   66
mixed species:
raw, meat only, 4 oz.   172
raw, 4 large shrimp (32 per lb.), meat only, 1
oz.   43
poached or steamed, meat only, 4 oz.   221
poached or steamed, 4 large shrimp   43
northern, raw, meat only, 4 oz.   142
canned or in jars:
dry-pack or drained solids, 4 oz.   196
dry-pack or drained solids, 1 cup   222
(*Sau-Sea*), 2.5 oz.   122

Shrimp, imitation:
    made from surimi, 4 oz.   41

Shrimp cocktail:
    with sauce, in jars *(Sau-Sea)*, 4 oz.   90

Shrimp dinner, frozen:
    baby, in sherried cream sauce *(Classic Lite)*,
        10½ oz.   110

Shrimp chow mein entrée:
    canned, drained *(Chun King Stir-Fry)*, 7.14 oz.   28

Sloppy Joe:
    canned *(Nalley's)*, 3½ oz.   15

Smelt:
    pond, raw, meat only, 4 oz.   82
    rainbow:
        raw, meat only, 4 oz.   79
        baked or broiled, meat only, 4 oz.   102
    sweet, raw, meat only, 4 oz.   28

Snail, see "Whelk"

Snapper:
    mixed species:
        raw, meat only, 4 oz.   42
        raw, 1 fillet, 7.7 oz. (from 3-lb. whole fish) . .   81
        baked or broiled, meat only, 4 oz.   53
        baked or broiled, 1 fillet, 6 oz. (7.7 oz. raw)   80

Snow peas, see "Peas, snow"

Soft drinks:
all varieties, canned or bottled   0

Sole:
European, raw, meat only, 4 oz.   57
mixed species:
    raw, meat only, 4 oz.   54
    raw, 1 fillet, 5.7 oz. (from 2-lb. whole fish) . .   78
    baked or broiled, meat only, 4 oz.   77
    baked or broiled, 1 fillet, 4.5 oz. (5.7 oz. raw)   86

Sorghum grain:
whole or ground   0

Soup, canned, ready-to-serve:
bean with ham, chunky, 19¼-oz. can   49
bean with ham, chunky, 1 cup   22
beef, chunky, 19-oz. can   32
beef, chunky, 1 cup.   14
beef broth or bouillon, 14-oz. can   1
beef broth or bouillon, 1 cup. . . . .   tr.
chicken, chunky, 10¾-oz. can   37
chicken, chunky, 1 cup   30
chicken noodle, 19-oz. can.   40
chicken noodle, 1 cup   18
chicken noodle with meatballs, 20-oz. can . . .   23
chicken noodle with meatballs, 1 cup   10
chicken rice, chunky, 19-oz. can   27
chicken rice, chunky, 1 cup   12
chicken vegetable, 19-oz. can.   38
chicken vegetable, 1 cup   17
clam chowder, Manhattan, 19-oz. can   32
clam chowder, Manhattan, 1 cup.   14
crab, 13-oz. can   10

Soup, canned, ready-to-serve *(cont.)*

crab, 1 cup	10
escarole, 19½-oz. can	6
escarole, 1 cup	2
gazpacho	0
lentil	0
lentil with ham, 20-oz. can	17
lentil with ham, 1 cup	7
minestrone, chunky, 19-oz. can	11
minestrone, chunky, 1 cup	5
pea, split, with ham, 19-oz. can	16
pea, split, with ham, 1 cup	7
turkey, chunky, 18¾-oz. can	21
turkey, chunky, 1 cup	9
vegetable, chunky	0

Soup, canned, condensed*

:

asparagus, cream of, 10¾-oz. can	12
asparagus, cream of, prepared with water, 1 cup	5
asparagus, cream of, prepared with whole milk, 1 cup	22
bean, black	0
bean with bacon, 11½-oz. can	6
bean with bacon, prepared with water, 1 cup	3
bean with frankfurter, 11¼-oz. can	29
bean with frankfurter, prepared with water, 1 cup	12
beef broth or bouillon, prepared with water, 1 cup	tr.

---

* *Prepared with equal amounts of soup and water or whole milk, as specified*

Soup, canned, condensed* *(cont.)*

beef mushroom, 10³/₄-oz. can	15
beef mushroom, prepared with water, 1 cup . .	7
beef noodle, 10³/₄-oz. can	12
beef noodle, prepared with water, 1 cup	5
beef vegetable, 10³/₄-oz. can	12
beef vegetable, prepared with water, 1 cup . . .	5
celery, cream of, 10³/₄-oz. can	34
celery, cream of, prepared with water, 1 cup . .	15
celery, cream of, prepared with whole milk, 1 cup	32
cheese, 11-oz. can	72
cheese, prepared with water, 1 cup	30
cheese, prepared with whole milk, 1 cup	48
chicken, cream of, 10³/₄-oz. can	24
chicken, cream of, prepared with water, 1 cup	10
chicken, cream of, prepared with whole milk, 1 cup	27
chicken alphabet, 10¹/₂-oz. can	15
chicken alphabet, prepared with water, 1 cup	7
chicken broth, 10³/₄-oz. can	3
chicken broth, prepared with water, 1 cup . . .	1
chicken and dumplings, 10¹/₂-oz. can	80
chicken and dumplings, prepared with water, 1 cup	34
chicken gumbo, 10³/₄-oz. can	9
chicken gumbo, prepared with water, 1 cup . .	5
chicken mushroom, 10³/₄-oz. can	24
chicken mushroom, prepared with water, 1 cup	10
chicken noodle, 10¹/₂-oz. can	15
chicken noodle, prepared with water, 1 cup . .	7

* Prepared with equal amounts of soup and water or whole milk, as specified

Soup, canned, condensed* *(cont.)*

chicken rice, 10½-oz. can	15
chicken rice, prepared with water, 1 cup	7
chicken with stars, 10½-oz. can	15
chicken with stars, prepared with water, 1 cup	7
chicken vegetable, 10½-oz. can	21
chicken vegetable, prepared with water, 1 cup	10
chili beef, 11¼-oz. can	32
chili beef, prepared with water, 1 cup	12
clam chowder:	
Manhattan, 10¾-oz. can	6
Manhattan, prepared with water, 1 cup	2
New England, 10¾-oz. can	12
New England, prepared with water, 1 cup . .	5
New England, prepared with whole milk, 1 cup	22
consommé, with gelatin	0
minestrone, 10½-oz. can	3
minestrone, prepared with water, 1 cup	2
mushroom, cream of, 10¾-oz. can	3
mushroom, cream of, prepared with water, 1 cup	2
mushroom, cream of, prepared with whole milk, 1 cup	20
mushroom barley	0
mushroom with beef stock, 10¾-oz. can	18
mushroom with beef stock, prepared with water	7
onion	0
onion, cream of, 10¾-oz. can	37
onion, cream of, prepared with water, 1 cup . .	15

---

* *Prepared with equal amount of soup and water or whole milk, as specified*

Soup, canned, condensed* *(cont.)*

onion, cream of, prepared with whole milk, 1 cup	32
oyster stew, 10½-oz. can	33
oyster stew, prepared with water, 1 cup	14
oyster stew, prepared with whole milk, 1 cup	32
pea, green	0
pea, green, prepared with whole milk, 1 cup	18
pea, split, with ham, 11½-oz. can	20
pea, split, with ham, prepared with water, 1 cup	8
pepperpot, 10½-oz. can	24
pepperpot, prepared with water, 1 cup	10
potato, cream of, 10¾-oz. can	15
potato, cream of, prepared with water, 1 cup	5
potato, cream of, prepared with whole milk, 1 cup	22
Scotch broth, 10½-oz. can	12
Scotch broth, prepared with water, 1 cup	5
shrimp, cream of, 10¾-oz. can	40
shrimp, cream of, prepared with water, 1 cup	17
shrimp, cream of, prepared with whole milk, 1 cup	35
stockpot, 11-oz. can	9
stockpot, prepared with water, 1 cup	5
tomato	0
tomato, prepared with whole milk, 1 cup	17
tomato beef with noodle, 10¾-oz. can	9
tomato beef with noodle, prepared with water, 1 cup	5
tomato bisque, 11-oz. can	11
tomato bisque, prepared with water, 1 cup	4

* Prepared with equal amount of soup and water or whole milk, as specified

Soup, canned, condensed* *(cont.)*

tomato bisque, prepared with whole milk, 1 cup	22
tomato rice, 11-oz. can	3
tomato rice, prepared with water, 1 cup	2
turkey noodle, 10¾-oz. can	12
turkey noodle, prepared with water, 1 cup . . .	5
turkey vegetable, 10½-oz. can	3
turkey vegetable, prepared with water, 1 cup	2
vegetable with beef, 10¾-oz. can	12
vegetable with beef, prepared with water, 1 cup	5
vegetable with beef broth, 10½-oz. can	6
vegetable with beef broth, prepared with water, 1 cup	2
vegetable, vegetarian	0

Soup, mix* :

asparagus, cream of, 1 cup	tr.
bean with bacon, 1 cup	3
beef broth or bouillon, 1 cup	1
beef and macaroni, 1 cup	2
beef noodle, 1 cup	2
beef flavored noodle, 1 cup	2
cauliflower, 1 cup	tr.
celery, cream of, 1 cup	1
chicken, cream of, 1 cup	3
chicken broth or bouillon, 1 cup	1
chicken noodle, 6 fl. oz.	2
chicken rice, 1 cup	3
chicken vegetable, 1 cup	3
clam chowder, Manhattan	0

---

* *Prepared with equal amounts of soup and water or whole milk, as specified*
** *Prepared according to package directions, with water*

Soup, mix *(cont.)*
clam chowder, New England, 1 cup   1
consommé   0
leek, 1 cup   2
minestrone, 1 cup   1
mushroom   0
onion   0
oxtail, 1 cup   2
pea, green or split, 1 cup   2
tomato, plain or cream of, 1 cup   1
tomato vegetable, 1 cup . . . .   tr.
vegetable, vegetarian   0

Soup greens:
(Durkee)   0

Sour cream, see "Cream"

Sour cream sauce mix:
dehydrated, 1.2-oz. pkg.   28
dehydrated, prepared with milk, 1 cup   91

Sour cocktail:
fluid or mix   0

Soursop:
fresh   0

Soybean:
green, raw or canned   0

Soybean, fermented:
natto or miso   0

Soybean curd:
tofu, all varieties 0

Soybean kernels:
raw, roasted, or toasted 0

Soybean lecithin:
soybean phosphatide and oil, granules or liquid 0

Soybean "milk":
fluid or powder 0

Soybean oil, see "Oil"

Soybean protein:
regular or proteinate 0

Soybean seeds:
mature, dry 0

Soy sauce:
(Chun King) 0
(Kikkoman/Kikkoman Lite), 1 tbsp. . . . . tr.

Spaghetti, see "Pasta"

Spaghetti, canned:
with meat or meatballs *(Nalley's),* 3½ oz. . . . 10

Spaghetti, mix* :
American style *(Kraft* Dinner) 0
Italian style *(Kraft* Dinner), 1 cup 5

---
* Prepared according to package directions

Spaghetti, mix *(cont.)*
with meat sauce *(Kraft Dinner)*, 1 cup   15

Spaghetti sauce:
canned or in jars:
(Ragu/Ragu Homestyle)   0
marinara *(Aunt Millie's)*, 1/2 cup . . . .   < 1
marinara *(Ragu)*   0
meat flavored *(Aunt Millie's)*, 1/2 cup   2
meat flavored *(Ragu* Extra Thick & Zesty), 4
oz.   2
meatless *(Aunt Millie's)*, 1/2 cup   2
mushroom *(Aunt Millie's)*, 1/2 cup . . . .   < 1
with mushrooms *(Ragu/Ragu* Homestyle) . .   0
pepper and mushroom *(Aunt Millie's)*, 1/2 cup   < 1
pepper and onion *(Aunt Millie's)*, 1/2 cup . . .   < 1
pepper and sausage *(Aunt Millie's)*, 1/2 cup   2
sausage *(Aunt Millie's)*, 1/2 cup   3

Spaghetti sauce mix:
dehydrated   0
dry *(Spatini)*   0
with mushrooms, dehydrated, 1.4-oz. pkg. . . .   11

Spanish mackerel, see "Mackerel"

Spareribs, see "Pork"

Spices, see specific listings

Spinach:
fresh or canned   0
frozen, without sauce   0

Spinach, New Zealand, see "New Zealand spinach"

Spiny lobster:

raw, meat only, 4 oz.	79
raw, meat only, 7.4 oz. (from 2-lb. whole lobster)	146

Spleen, fresh:

beef, raw, 4 oz.	298
beef, braised, 4 oz.	393
beef, braised, 10.9 oz. (yield from 1 lb. raw)	1069
pork, raw, 4 oz.	410
pork, braised, 4 oz.	572
pork, braised, 10.6 oz. (yield from 1 lb. raw)	1506

Sports drink:

(Max)	0

Sprat:

raw, meat only, 4 oz.	43

Squab:

raw, meat only, 4 oz.	102
raw, breast meat only, 1 breast, 3.6 oz.	91

Squash:

all varieties, summer or winter, fresh or canned	0
all varieties, summer or winter, frozen, without sauce	0

Squash seed kernels:

raw or dried	0

Squid:
  mixed species, fresh:
    raw, meat only, 4 oz. 264
    flour-coated, fried in vegetable shortening, 4
    oz. 295

Steak, see "Beef" and "Salisbury steak dinner"

Steak sauce:
  (A.1) 0
  (Escoffier Sauce Diable/Sauce Robert) 0
  (Heinz 57) 0
  (Heublein Steak Supreme) 0
  (Lea & Perrins) 0

Stomach, pork, see "Pork stomach"

Strawberries:
  fresh or frozen 0

Strawberry juice or drink:
  canned or mix 0

Strawberry roll or bar:
  natural or sweetened 0

Stroganoff sauce mix:
  dehydrated, 1.6-oz. pkg. 12
  dehydrated, prepared with milk and water, 1
    cup 38

Stuffing mix:
  dry type. 0

Stuffing mix *(cont.)*
　moist type, 1 cup* . . . . 　67

Succotash:
　fresh or canned . . . . 　0
　frozen, without sauce . . . . 　0

Sucker:
　white:
　　raw, meat only, 4 oz. . . . . 　46
　　raw, 1 fillet, 5.6 oz. (from 2 lb. whole fish) . . 　56

Suet:
　raw, 1 oz. . . . . 　19

Sugar:
　beet or cane, all varieties . . . . 　0

Sugar, maple:
　canned or in jars . . . . 　0

Sugar apple (sweetsop):
　fresh . . . . 　0

Sugar substitute:
　all varieties . . . . 　0

Sukiyaki entrée:
　canned *(Chun King* Stir-Fry), 6 oz. . . . . 　52

Summer sausage (see also "Thuringer
　　cervelat"):
————
* *Prepared according to package directions, with egg*

Summer sausage *(cont.)*
   (Oscar Mayer), .82-oz. slice   17
   beef *(Oscar Mayer)*, .82-oz. slice   17
   cheese *(Armour)*, 1 oz.   20

Sunfish:
   pumpkinseed:
      raw, meat only, 4 oz.   76
      raw, 1 fillet, 1.7 oz. (from 3/4-lb. whole fish)   32

Sunflower butter:
   raw, unsalted *(Hain)*   0

Sunflower nuts:
   dry or oil-roasted   0

Sunflower seed oil, see "Oil"

Sunflower seed flour:
   partially defatted   0

Sunflower seeds:
   dry or roasted   0

Surimi:
   processed from walleye pollock, 4 oz.   34

Surinam cherry, see "Pitanga"

Swamp cabbage:
   fresh   0

Sweet and sour cocktail:
   fluid or mix   0

Sweet and sour sauce:
  bottled   0
  dehydrated mix, prepared with water and
    vinegar   0

Sweetsop, see "Sugar apple"

Sweetbreads, hog, see "Pork pancreas"

Sweet potato:
  fresh or dehydrated   0
  candied, fresh, canned, or frozen   0

Sweet potato leaves:
  fresh   0

Swordfish:
  raw, meat only, 4 oz.   44
  raw, 1 steak (4¹/₂″ × 2¹/₈″ × ⁷/₈″), 4.8 oz. . .   54
  baked or broiled, meat only, 4 oz.   57
  baked or broiled, 1 steak, 3.7 oz. (4.8 oz. raw)   53

Syrup (see also specific listings):
  (Knotts)   0

T

Food and Measure	Cholesterol (mgs.)
Tabouly mix:	
dry *(Casbah)*	0
Taco dip:	
(Hain Taco Dip & Sauce)	0
(Thank You), 2 tbsp.	1
Taco sauce:	
all varieties *(Del Monte)*	0
all varieties *(Ortega)*	0
Taco seasoning mix*:	
mild *(Ortega)*, 1 oz.	18
Tahini, see "Sesame paste"	

* *Prepared according to package directions, with ground beef*

Tallow:
beef, 1 cup	223
beef, 1 tbsp.	14
mutton, 1 cup	209
mutton, 1 tbsp.	13

Tamale pie:
canned *(Nalley's)*, 3½ oz.	15

Tamarind:
fresh	0

Tangelo:
fresh	0

Tangerine:
fresh or canned	0

Tangerine juice:
fresh, canned, or frozen	0

Taro:
all varieties, raw	0

Taro chips:
dehydrated	0

Taro leaves:
raw	0

Taro shoots:
raw	0

Tarragon:
fresh or dried   0

Tartar sauce:
(Best Foods/Hellmann's), 1 tbsp.   5
(Kraft), 1 tbsp.   5
(Nalley's), 1 tbsp.   9
(Sauceworks), 1 tbsp.   5

Tea:
all varieties, regular or herbal, plain   0

Teaseed oil, see "Oil"

Tendergreens, see "Mustard spinach"

Tequila, see "Liquor"

Teriyaki sauce:
(Kikkoman), 1 tbsp.   tr.
(Kikkoman Baste and Glaze)   0
dehydrated mix, prepared with water   0

Thuringer cervelat (see also "Summer
sausage"):
beef and pork, 1 oz.   19
beef and pork, 1 slice (10 per 8-oz. pkg.)   16

Thyme:
fresh or dried   0

Thymus, see "Beef thymus"

Tofu, see "Soybean curd"

Tofu entrées, frozen:
cannelloni Florentine *(Legume)* 0
enchilada, Mexican *(Legume)* 0
lasagna *(Legume Classic)* 0
manicotti *(Legume Classic)* 0
pepper steak, whole wheat noodles *(Legume)* 0
sesame ginger stir-fry, brown rice *(Legume)*,
   11½ oz. 1
shells, stuffed, Provençale *(Legume)* 0
sweet and sour, whole wheat noodles
   (Legume) 0

Tom Collins cocktail:
fluid or mix. 0

Tomato:
green or ripe, fresh or canned 0

Tomato paste or puree:
fresh, canned, or in jars 0

Tomato, pickled:
canned or in jars 0

Tomato juice:
canned or dehydrated 0

Tomato sauce:
meatless, canned or in jars 0

Tomato seed oil, see "Oil"

Tongue:
  beef:
    raw, 4 oz.   98
    braised or simmered, 4 oz.   121
    braised or simmered, 9.1 oz. (yield from 1 lb.
      raw)   278
  pork:
    raw, 4 oz.   114
    braised or simmered, 4 oz.   166
    braised or simmered, 8.1 oz. (yield from 1 lb.
      raw)   371

Toppings, dessert:
  all varieties, except cream   0
  cream or whipped, see "Cream" and "Cream,
    imitation" . . . .
  marshmallow creme   0

Tortilla chips:
  regular or barbecue flavor   0

Towel gourd, see "Gourd"

Tripe, see "Beef tripe"

Trout:
  mixed species:
    raw, meat only, 4 oz.   66
    raw, 1 fillet, 2.8 oz. (from 1-lb. whole fish) . .   46
  rainbow:
    raw, meat only, 4 oz.   65
    raw, 1 fillet, 2.8 oz. (from 1-lb. whole fish) . .   45
    baked or broiled, meat only, 4 oz.   83
    baked or broiled, 1 fillet, 2.2 oz. (2.8 oz. raw)   45

Trout, sea, see "Sea trout"

Tuna:
  fresh:
    bluefin, raw, meat only, 4 oz. 43
    bluefin, baked or broiled, meat only, 4 oz. . . 56
    skipjack, raw, meat only, 4 oz. 53
    yellowfin, raw, meat only, 4 oz. 51
  canned in oil:
    light, chunk *(Bumble Bee),* 2 oz. 30
    light, solid or chunk *(Star-Kist),* 2 oz. 31
    white, solid *(Bumble Bee),* 2 oz. 30
    white, solid or chunk *(Star-Kist),* 2 oz. 31
  canned in water:
    light, chunk *(Bumble Bee),* 2 oz. 30
    light, solid or chunk *(Star-Kist),* 2 oz. 27
    white, drained, 2 oz. 24
    white, solid, albacore *(Star-Kist),* 2 oz. 27

Tuna salad:
  with mayonnaise-type dressing, 1/2 cup 14

Turf and surf dinner:
  frozen *(Classic Lite),* 10 oz. 80

Turkey, edible portions:
  fryer-roaster, raw:
    meat and skin, 10.9 oz. (yield per 1 lb. with
      bone) 252
  fryer-roaster, roasted:
    meat and skin, 8.1 oz. (yield per 1 lb. raw
      with bone) 241
    meat and skin, 1/2 turkey (2.4 lbs. with bone) 849
    meat and skin, 4 oz. 119

Turkey, fryer-roaster, roasted *(cont.)*

meat only, 4 oz.	111
meat only, chopped or diced, 1 cup or 4.9 oz.	138
dark meat only, 4 oz.	127
light meat only, 4 oz.	98
skin only, 1 oz.	41
breast, with skin, 1/2 breast (13.7 oz. with bone)	310
breast, meat only, 1/2 breast	255
leg, with skin, 1 leg (11.4 oz. with bone)	267
leg, meat only, 1 leg	171
wing, with skin, 1 wing (5.2 oz. with bone)	104
wing, meat only, 1 wing	61

giblets, see "Giblets"

pre-basted with turkey broth (see also "Turkey, frozen"):

roasted, 1/2 breast, with skin (2.1 lbs. with bone)	359
roasted, 1 thigh, with skin (12.7 oz. with bone)	194

young hen, raw:

meat and skin, 11.5 oz. (yield per 1 lb. with bone)	206

young hen, roasted:

meat and skin, 8.6 oz. (yield per 1 lb. raw with bone)	190
meat and skin, 1/2 turkey (4.2 lbs. with bone)	1,190
meat and skin, 4 oz.	88
meat only, 4 oz.	83
meat only, chopped or diced, 1 cup or 4.9 oz.	102
dark meat only, 4 oz.	96
light meat only, 4 oz.	77

Turkey, young hen, roasted *(cont.)*
   skin only, 1 oz.   30
   breast, with skin, 1/2 breast (1.6 lbs. with
      bone) 492
   leg, with skin, 1 leg (1.2 lbs. with bone) 365
   wing, with skin, 1 wing (8.9 oz. with bone) . . 134
  young tom, raw:
   meat and skin, 11.9 oz. (yield per 1 lb. with
      bone) 243
  young tom, roasted:
   meat and skin, 8.4 oz. (yield per 1 lb. raw
      with bone) 197
   meat and skin, 1/2 turkey (7.6 lbs. with bone) 2,265
   meat and skin, 4 oz.   93
   meat only, 4 oz.   87
   meat only, chopped or diced, 1 cup or 4.9
      oz. 108
   dark meat only, 4 oz. 100
   light meat only, 4 oz.   78
   skin only, 1 oz.   33
   breast, with skin, 1/2 breast (3.2 lbs. with
      bone) 1,002
   leg, with skin, 1 leg (2.2 lbs. with bone) 727
   wing, with skin, 1 wing (13.3 oz. with bone) 192

Turkey, frozen:
  breast *(Land O Lakes)*, 3 oz.   50
  broth baste, young *(Land O Lakes* Self-
    Basting), 3 oz.   77
  butter baste *(Land O Lakes)*, 3 oz.   85
  cured, breast *(Armour)*, 4 oz.   65
  light meat, with gravy *(Armour Star)*, 3.7 oz. . .   50
  light and dark meat, with gravy *(Armour Star)*,
    3.7 oz.   50

Turkey, frozen (cont.)

roasted, light meat, no skin:

    10–12-lb. hen (Beatrice Butterball), 3½ oz.   80

    14–16-lb. tom (Beatrice Butterball), 3½ oz.   80

roasted, dark meat, no skin:

    10–12-lb. hen (Beatrice Butterball), 3½ oz.   125

    14–16-lb. tom (Beatrice Butterball), 3½ oz.   130

roasted, light and dark meat and skin:

    10–12-lb. hen (Beatrice Butterball), 3½ oz.   95

    14–16-lb. tom (Beatrice Butterball), 3½ oz.   100

    seasoned, 1.7-lb. box   413

roasted, skin only:

    10–12-lb. hen (Beatrice Butterball), 3½ oz.   140

    14–16-lb. tom (Beatrice Butterball), 3½ oz.   135

Turkey, sliced and luncheon meat:

bologna, see "Turkey bologna"

breast, ¾-oz. slice (8 per 6-oz. pkg.)   9

breast (Louis Rich), 1 oz.   12

breast, slices (Louis Rich), 1 slice   13

breast, tenderloin (Louis Rich), 1 oz.   9

breast, with cheese (Land O Lakes), 5 oz. . . .   35

butter added (Golden Star), 4 oz.   68

ground (Louis Rich), 1 oz.   24

loaf (Louis Rich), 1-oz. slice   43

ham, see "Turkey ham"

pastrami, see "Turkey pastrami"

salami, see "Turkey salami"

smoked:

    (Carl Buddig), 1 oz.   6

    (Louis Rich), 1-oz. slice   12

    breast (Louis Rich), 1 oz.   13

    breast (Oscar Mayer), ¾-oz. slice   7

    breast, chunk (Louis Rich), 1 oz.   11

Turkey, sliced and luncheon meat, smoked *(cont.)*
  breast, sliced *(Louis Rich)*, .7-oz. slice   7
  with barbecue sauce *(Armour Star)*, 4 oz. . .   50
  with spiced sauce *(Armour Star)*, 4 oz.   50
  light meat:
    with gravy *(Armour Star)*, 4 oz.   50
    roast, with gravy *(Land O Lakes* Buttermoist)*,
      3 oz.   20
    roll, 1-oz. slice   12
    roll *(Avondale)*, 3 oz.   45
    roll *(Gold Band)*, 3 oz.   45
    roll *(Land O Lakes* Blue Label)*, 3 oz.   50
    roll *(Land O Lakes* Red Label)*, 3 oz.   50
    roll *(Magic Slice)*, 3 oz.   50
  light and dark meat:
    diced *(Land O Lakes)*, 3 oz.   35
    with gravy *(Armour Star)*, 4 oz.   50
    roast, with gravy *(Land O Lakes* Buttermoist)*,
      3 oz.   20
    roll, 1-oz. slice   16
    roll *(Avondale)*, 3 oz.   50
    roll *(Gold Band)*, 3 oz.   50
    roll *(Land O Lakes* Red Label)*, 3 oz.   50
    roll *(Magic Slice)*, 3 oz.   50
  with dressing and gravy *(Armour Star)*, 4 oz. . . .   35

Turkey bologna:
  1-oz. slice   28
  (Armour), 4 oz.   95
  (Louis Rich), 1-oz. slice   19

Turkey-chicken salad, see "Poultry salad"

Turkey dinner, frozen:
Dijon *(Lean Cuisine)*, 9½ oz. 70
Parmesan *(Classic Lite)*, 11 oz. 70

Turkey fat:
raw, ½ cup 105
raw, 1 tbsp. 13

Turkey frankfurter:
1 oz. 30
1.6-oz. link 48
(Armour Star), 2-oz. link 50
(Louis Rich), 1 link 39
cheese *(Louis Rich)*, 1 link 40

Turkey giblets, see "Giblets"

Turkey gizzard, see "Gizzard"

Turkey gravy:
canned, 10½-oz. can 6
canned, 1 cup 5
dehydrated mix, prepared with water, 1 cup . . 3

Turkey ham:
(Armour), 1 oz. 15
(Louis Rich/Louis Rich Water Added), 1 oz. . . 21
chopped *(Louis Rich)*, 1 oz. 17

Turkey heart, see "Heart"

Turkey liver, see "Liver"

Turkey meat loaf:
(*Armour*), 3 oz. 50

Turkey pastrami:
(*Armour*), 1 oz. 13

Turkey patties:
(*Land O Lakes*), 2 1/4 oz. 30

Turkey salami:
(*Louis Rich*), 1-oz. slice 19
cooked, 1-oz. slice 23
cotto (*Armour*), 1 oz. 18
cotto (*Louis Rich*), 1-oz. slice 22

Turkey sausage:
breakfast (*Louis Rich*), 1 oz. 23
smoked (*Louis Rich*), 1 oz. 19

Turkey sticks:
(*Land O Lakes*), 2 sticks or 2 oz. 25

Turmeric:
ground 0

Turnip:
fresh 0
frozen, without sauce 0

Turnip greens:
fresh, canned, or frozen 0

V

Food and Measure	Cholesterol (mgs.)

Vanilla extract:
  pure (*Virginia Dare*)   0

Veal, edible portions:
  cutlet, medium fat:
    raw, 4 oz.   115
    braised or broiled, 4 oz.   124
    braised or broiled, 1 cutlet, 4$\frac{1}{8}$″ × 2$\frac{1}{4}$″
      × $\frac{1}{2}$″   109
  leg, round with rump, raw, 4 oz.   81
  rib, medium fat:
    braised or broiled, 4 oz.   124
    braised or broiled, 1 piece, 4$\frac{1}{8}$″ × 2$\frac{1}{4}$″
      × $\frac{1}{4}$″   55

Veal Parmigiana dinner:
  frozen (*Dinner Classics*), 10$\frac{3}{4}$ oz.   85

Vegetable juice:
    all blends, canned or in jars   0

Vegetable seasoning:
    (*Lawry's Natural Choice* for Vegetables)   0

Vegetables, mixed:
    all varieties, fresh or canned   0
    all varieties, frozen, without sauce   0

Vegetarian foods (see also specific listings):
    all varieties, canned, dried, or frozen   0

Venison:
    raw, lean meat only, 4 oz.   76

Vine spinach:
    fresh   0

Vinegar:
    all varieties   0

Vodka, see "Liquor"

W

Waffles:
  mix, prepared with egg and milk, 1 waffle, 7″
    diam.   59

Walnut:
  all varieties, raw or dried   0

Walnut oil, see "Oil"

Water chestnuts:
  Chinese, fresh or canned   0

Watercress:
  fresh   0

Watermelon:
  fresh   0

Watermelon rind:
  pickled   0

Watermelon seed kernels:
  raw or dried   0

Wax gourd (Chinese preserving melon):
  fresh   0

Weiners, see "Frankfurters and Weiners"

Wendy's:
  breakfast, 1 serving:
    bacon, 2 strips   15
    breakfast sandwich, 4.6 oz.   200
    eggs, scrambled, 3.25 oz.   450
    French toast, 2 slices   115
    home fries, 3.7 oz.   20
    omelet:
      ham and cheese, 4 oz.   450
      ham, cheese & mushroom, 4.2 oz.   355
      ham, cheese, onion, green pepper, 4.6 oz.   525
      mushroom, onion, green pepper, 4 oz. . . .   460
    sausage, 1 patty   30
    toast with margarine   0
  chili, 8 oz.   30
  sandwiches, 1 serving:
    bacon cheeseburger, white bun, 5.25 oz. . . .   65
    chicken, wheat bun, 4.6 oz.   59
    hamburger:
      single, wheat bun, 4.25 oz.   67

Wendy's, sandwiches , hamburger*(cont.)*

    single, white bun, 4.2 oz. 65

    double, white bun, 7 oz. 125

    Kids' Meal, 2.7 oz. 20

    condiments:

      American cheese, .6-oz. slice 15

      bacon, 3½ slices 10

      dill pickle or relish 0

      ketchup or mustard 0

      lettuce, tomato, or onion rings 0

      mayonnaise, 1 tbsp. 10

    baked potato, hot, stuffed, 1 serving:

      plain, 8.8 oz. 1

      bacon and cheese, 12.5 oz. 22

      broccoli and cheese, 13 oz. 22

      cheese, 12.5 oz. 22

      chicken à la king, 12.8 oz. 20

      chili and cheese, 14.2 oz. 22

      sour cream and chives, 11 oz. 15

      Stroganoff and sour cream, 14.5 oz. 43

    salads and side dishes, 1 serving:

      French fries, regular, 3.5 oz. 15

      pick-up window side salad, 18.2 oz. 15

      taco salad, 12.75 oz. 40

    dessert, dairy, frosty, 12 fl. oz. 50

Wheat, parboiled, see "Bulgur"

Wheat, whole-grain:

    all varieties 0

Wheat bran:

    crude, processed, or toasted 0

Wheat germ:
crude or processed   0
honey (*Kretschmer*)   0

Wheat germ oil, see "Oil"

Wheat nuts:
(*Flavor Tree*)   0

Wheat pilaf mix:
dry (*Casbah*)   0

Whelk:
raw, meat only, 4 oz.   74
boiled or steamed, meat only, 4 oz.   147

Whey:
sweet, fluid, 1/2 cup   3
sweet, fluid, 1 oz.   < 1
sweet, dry, 1/2 cup   5
sweet, dry, 1 oz.   2
sweet, dry or fluid, 1 tbsp. . . . .   tr.

Whiskey, see "Liquor"

Whiskey sour cocktail:
fluid or mix   0

White sauce mix:
dehydrated, 1.8-oz. pkg. . . . .   tr.
dehydrated, prepared with whole milk, yield
from 1 pkg.   86
dehydrated, prepared with whole milk, 1 cup . .   34

Whitefish:
mixed species, fresh:
raw, meat only, 4 oz. 68
raw, 1 fillet, 7 oz. (from 2½-lb. whole fish) . . 119
smoked, meat only, 4 oz. 37

Whiting:
mixed species:
raw, meat only, 4 oz. 76
raw, 1 fillet, 3.2 oz. (from 1½-lb. whole fish) 61
baked or broiled, meat only, 4 oz. 95
baked or broiled, 1 fillet, 3 oz. (3.2 oz. raw) 60

Wine:
all varieties, cooking, fortified, table, or
sparkling 0

Winged bean:
raw 0

Winged bean tuber:
raw 0

Wolf fish:
Atlantic:
raw, meat only, 4 oz. 52
raw, ½ fillet, 5.4 oz. (from 5-lb. whole fish) 70

Worcestershire sauce:
(*French's*) 0
(*Lea & Perrins*) 0

Y

Food and Measure	Cholesterol (mgs.)

Yam, see "Sweet potato"

Yam bean:
    tuber, raw or boiled 0

Yardlong bean:
    raw or boiled 0

Yeast:
    bakers, all varieties 0
    brewer's, all varieties 0

Yogurt:
    plain:
        (*Columbo*), 8 oz. 15
        (*Columbo* Natural Lite), 8 oz. 2
        (*Dannon* Lowfat), 8 oz. 12

Yogurt, plain *(cont.)*

whole milk, 8 oz.	29
whole milk, 6 oz.	22
lowfat, 8 oz.	14
lowfat, 6 oz.	10
skim milk, 8 oz.	4
skim milk, 6 oz.	3
apple, Dutch (*Dannon* Lowfat), 8 oz.	< 11
banana (*Dannon* Lowfat), 8 oz.	< 11
banana-strawberry (*Columbo*), 8 oz.	20
berry:	
mixed (*Dannon* Lowfat), 8 oz.	< 11
mixed (*Dannon* Hearty Nuts & Raisins), 8 oz.	9
mixed (*Dannon* Y.E.S.), 6 oz.	< 9
wild (*Columbo*), 8 oz.	20
blueberry:	
(*Columbo*), 8 oz.	20
(*Dannon* Lowfat), 8 oz.	< 11
(*Dannon* Y.E.S.), 6 oz.	< 9
boysenberry (*Dannon* Lowfat), 8 oz.	< 11
cherry (*Dannon* Lowfat), 8 oz.	< 11
cherry (*Dannon* Y.E.S.), 6 oz.	< 9
cherry-vanilla (*Columbo*), 8 oz.	20
coffee:	
(*Dannon* Lowfat), 8 oz.	< 11
lowfat, 8 oz.	11
lowfat, 6 oz.	9
fruit, lowfat, 8 oz.	10
fruit, 6 oz.	7
granola (*Columbo* Breakfast), 8 oz.	20
honey vanilla (*Columbo*), 8 oz.	20
lemon (*Columbo*), 8 oz.	20
lemon (*Dannon* Lowfat), 8 oz.	< 11

Yogurt, coffee *(cont.)*
    orchard fruits (*Dannon* Hearty Nuts &
      Raisins), 8 oz.   9
   peach:
    (*Dannon* Lowfat), 8 oz. . . . . < 11
    (*Dannon* Y.E.S.), 6 oz. . . . . < 9
    Melba (*Columbo*), 8 oz. 20
   piña colada:
    (*Columbo*), 8 oz. 20
    (*Dannon* Lowfat), 8 oz. . . . . < 11
    (*Dannon* Y.E.S.), 6 oz. . . . . < 9
   raspberry:
    (*Columbo*), 8 oz. 20
    (*Dannon* Lowfat), 8 oz. . . . . < 11
    (*Dannon* Y.E.S.), 6 oz. . . . . < 9
   strawberry:
    (*Columbo*), 8 oz. 20
    (*Dannon* Lowfat), 8 oz. . . . . < 11
    (*Dannon* Y.E.S.), 6 oz. . . . . < 9
   strawberry-banana (*Dannon* Lowfat), 8 oz. . . . < 11
   strawberry-banana (*Dannon* Y.E.S.), 6 oz. . . . . < 9
   strawberry-vanilla (*Columbo*), 8 oz. 20
   vanilla:
    (*Dannon* Lowfat), 8 oz. . . . . < 11
    (*Dannon* Hearty Nuts & Raisins), 8 oz. 9
    French (*Columbo*), 8 oz. 20
    lowfat, 8 oz. 11
    lowfat, 6 oz. 9

Z

Food and Measure	Cholesterol (mgs.)

Ziti, see "Pasta"

Zucchini:
   fresh or frozen, see "Squash"
   canned in tomato sauce 0